WHO AM I?

Kindergarten Workbook

WHO AM I?

Kindergarten Workbook

Second Edition

First Edition Authors

Mary Jo Smith and Jerelyn Helmberger

Revision Author

Mary Jo Smith

*Educational
and
Theological Advisors*

Most Rev. John M. LeVoir
Mary Jo Smith

IMAGE OF GOD SERIES

IMAGE OF GOD, INC., CRYSTAL, MN

IGNATIUS PRESS   SAN FRANCISCO

Nihil obstat: Reverend Joseph Johnson
                    Censor Librorum

Imprimatur: ✠ Most Reverend John C. Nienstedt
                    Archbishop of St. Paul and Minneapolis
                    March 31, 2012

For teacher information go to www.ipreligioused.com

Cover design by Riz Boncan Marsella
Cover and text illustrations by Barbara Harasyn

2022 reprint
First Edition published 1991 by Ignatius Press, San Francisco
Second Edition published 2012 by Ignatius Press, San Francisco
© 2014 by Image of God, Inc., Crystal, MN
All rights reserved
ISBN: 978-1-58617-372-2
Printed by Friesens Corporation in Altona, MB, Canada on March 2022
Job Number 283306
In compliance with the Consumer Protection Safety Act, 2008

CONTENTS

LETTER TO PARENTS OR GUARDIANS

Dear Parents or Guardians,

This year your child will be using the "Who Am I?" kindergarten curriculum from the *Image of God* series. This series is centered on the subjective turn found in the writings and teachings of Saint John Paul II. This subjective turn stresses the dignity of each individual as a person made in the image of God. Because we are images of God we possess a great dignity. This also means that the better we know God, the better we will know ourselves. Your child will more deeply come to understand this through studying this curriculum.

The kindergarten program has as its focus two key ideas: God and creation. These key ideas, along with an emphasis on Sacred Scripture, form the unifying element of the lessons.

You, as parents or guardians, are the primary religious educators of your children. With this in mind, the "Who Am I?" curriculum has take-home materials which provide a basis for faith discussions at home with your child. There is a set of worksheets for most lessons. Sometimes your child will bring home a completed worksheet to share. Sometimes, though, it will be up to you, as parents, to complete the worksheet with your child.

On the back of the worksheets you will find Family Notes. These contain the Scripture reference for the lesson's Bible story, which has been adapted for children; an explanation of the main focus of the lesson, providing you with background to discuss the lesson with your child; the concept of faith that was the foundation of the lesson, presented in a question-and-answer format; a Correspondence to the *Catechism of the Catholic Church* section that lists topics taught in the lesson and that provides references to the corresponding paragraphs in the *Catechism of the Catholic Church*; and a suggested home activity for you and your child.

It is our hope that through this program you and your child will grow in faith together.

Directions: Count the persons. Circle the correct number.

1 2 3 4 5

1 2 3 4 5

1 2 3 4 5

1 2 3 4 5

There are three persons in one God.

Family Note

Lesson 1: There Is One God—The Blessed Trinity

In this lesson the Sign of the Cross and the Glory Be are introduced. Each time we make the Sign of the Cross we give praise to the three persons of the Blessed Trinity. When we say the Glory Be, we are showing that we believe that God always was and always will be.

Vocabulary

Blessed Trinity: we call the three persons in one God the Blessed Trinity
mystery: something we cannot fully understand

Concepts of Faith

How many Gods are there?
There is one God, and there are three persons in the one God: Father, Son, and Holy Spirit.

What do we call the three persons in one God?
We call the three persons in one God the Blessed Trinity.

Correspondence to the *Catechism of the Catholic Church*

Belief in one God: *CCC* 199–202, 228
The implications of faith in one God: *CCC* 222–27, 229
"In the name of the Father and of the Son and of the Holy Spirit": *CCC* 232–37, 265
The revelation of God as the Blessed Trinity: *CCC* 238–48, 261–64
Blessed Trinity in the teaching of the faith: *CCC* 249–56, 266
The divine works and the trinitarian missions: *CCC* 257–60, 267

Suggested Activity

Review the Sign of the Cross and the Glory Be with your child:

Glory be to the Father
and to the Son, and to the Holy Spirit,
as it was in the beginning, is now,
and ever shall be, world without end. Amen.

Directions: Cut out the puzzle pieces. Put the puzzle together.

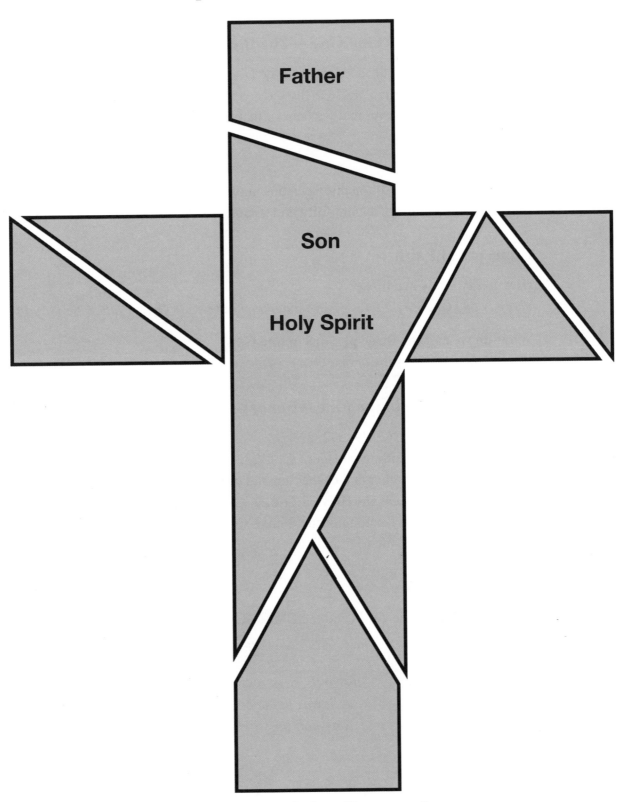

Father

Son

Holy Spirit

We make the Sign of the Cross when we pray.

Family Note

Lesson 1: There Is One God—The Blessed Trinity

In this lesson the Sign of the Cross and the Glory Be are introduced. Each time we make the Sign of the Cross we give praise to the three persons of the Blessed Trinity. When we say the Glory Be, we are showing that we believe that God always was and always will be.

Vocabulary

Blessed Trinity: we call the three persons in one God the Blessed Trinity
mystery: something we cannot fully understand

Concepts of Faith

How many Gods are there?
There is one God, and there are three persons in the one God: Father, Son, and Holy Spirit.

What do we call the three persons in one God?
We call the three persons in one God the Blessed Trinity.

Correspondence to the *Catechism of the Catholic Church*

Belief in one God: *CCC* 199–202, 228
The implications of faith in one God: *CCC* 222–27, 229
"In the name of the Father and of the Son and of the Holy Spirit": *CCC* 232–37, 265
The revelation of God as the Blessed Trinity: *CCC* 238–48, 261–64
Blessed Trinity in the teaching of the faith: *CCC* 249–56, 266
The divine works and the trinitarian missions: *CCC* 257–60, 267

Suggested Activity

Review the Sign of the Cross and the Glory Be with your child:

Glory be to the Father
and to the Son, and to the Holy Spirit,
as it was in the beginning, is now,
and ever shall be, world without end. Amen.

Directions: Cut out the pictures. Put them in the correct order.

as it was in the beginning, is now, and ever shall be, world without end. Amen.

Glory be to the Father,

and to the Holy Spirit,

and to the Son,

Family Note

Lesson 1: There Is One God—The Blessed Trinity

In this lesson the Sign of the Cross and the Glory Be are introduced. Each time we make the Sign of the Cross we give praise to the three persons of the Blessed Trinity. When we say the Glory Be, we are showing that we believe that God always was and always will be.

Vocabulary

Blessed Trinity: we call the three persons in one God the Blessed Trinity
mystery: something we cannot fully understand

Concepts of Faith

How many Gods are there?
There is one God, and there are three persons in the one God: Father, Son, and Holy Spirit.

What do we call the three persons in one God?
We call the three persons in one God the Blessed Trinity.

Correspondence to the *Catechism of the Catholic Church*

Belief in one God: *CCC* 199–202, 228
The implications of faith in one God: *CCC* 222–27, 229
"In the name of the Father and of the Son and of the Holy Spirit": *CCC* 232–37, 265
The revelation of God as the Blessed Trinity: *CCC* 238–48, 261–64
Blessed Trinity in the teaching of the faith: *CCC* 249–56, 266
The divine works and the trinitarian missions: *CCC* 257–60, 267

Suggested Activity

Review the Sign of the Cross and the Glory Be with your child:

Glory be to the Father
and to the Son, and to the Holy Spirit,
as it was in the beginning, is now,
and ever shall be, world without end. Amen.

Directions: Count God's creations. Draw a line to the correct number.

7

8

6

9

5

God made everything from nothing.

Family Note

Lesson 2: We See God in the World around Us—Creation

The story for this lesson is an adaptation of Genesis 1:1–31. We call God Creator because he made the world and everything in it from nothing. God made all the things in the world for people to use. We can use all the things God made, but we cannot use other people. We love, praise, and thank God for the wonderful world he has given us.

Vocabulary

Creator: God, who made everything from nothing
angels: persons created by God without bodies

Concepts of Faith

Who made the world and everything in it?
God made the world and everything in it.

Who is our Creator?
God is our Creator.

Who are the angels?
The angels are persons but they do not have bodies. They praise God, and act as God's messengers and our guardians.

Correspondence to the *Catechism of the Catholic Church*

The Creator: *CCC* 279–81
Catechesis on creation: *CCC* 282–89
The world was created for the glory of God: *CCC* 293–94, 319
The mystery of creation: *CCC* 295–301, 317–18, 320
Man created in the image of God: *CCC* 355–57, 380–81

Suggested Activity

Go for a walk with your child. Point out all the wonderful things God has given us.

Directions: Draw a line from God's creations to their shadows.

God made the whole world and everything in it.

Family Note

Lesson 2: We See God in the World around Us—Creation

The story for this lesson is an adaptation of Genesis 1:1–31. We call God Creator because he made the world and everything in it from nothing. God made all the things in the world for people to use. We can use all the things God made, but we cannot use other people. We love, praise, and thank God for the wonderful world he has given us.

Vocabulary

Creator: God, who made everything from nothing
angels: persons created by God without bodies

Concepts of Faith

Who made the world and everything in it?
God made the world and everything in it.

Who is our Creator?
God is our Creator.

Who are the angels?
The angels are persons but they do not have bodies. They praise God, and act as God's messengers and our guardians.

Correspondence to the *Catechism of the Catholic Church*

The Creator: *CCC* 279–81
Catechesis on creation: *CCC* 282–89
The world was created for the glory of God: *CCC* 293–94, 319
The mystery of creation: *CCC* 295–301, 317–18, 320
Man created in the image of God: *CCC* 355–57, 380–81

Suggested Activity

Go for a walk with your child. Point out all the wonderful things God has given us.

Directions: *Match the mothers and their babies.*

All life comes from God.

Family Note

Lesson 2: We See God in the World around Us—Creation

The story for this lesson is an adaptation of Genesis 1:1–31. We call God Creator because he made the world and everything in it from nothing. God made all the things in the world for people to use. We can use all the things God made, but we cannot use other people. We love, praise, and thank God for the wonderful world he has given us.

Vocabulary

Creator: God, who made everything from nothing
angels: persons created by God without bodies

Concepts of Faith

Who made the world and everything in it?
God made the world and everything in it.

Who is our Creator?
God is our Creator.

Who are the angels?
The angels are persons but they do not have bodies. They praise God, and act as God's messengers and our guardians.

Correspondence to the *Catechism of the Catholic Church*

The Creator: *CCC* 279–81
Catechesis on creation: *CCC* 282–89
The world was created for the glory of God: *CCC* 293–94, 319
The mystery of creation: *CCC* 295–301, 317–18, 320
Man created in the image of God: *CCC* 355–57, 380–81

Suggested Activity

Go for a walk with your child. Point out all the wonderful things God has given us.

Directions: Find and color the hidden animals.

God asked Adam to name all the animals.

Family Note

Lesson 3: I Am Special to God, Who Made Me

The two stories for this lesson are adaptations of Luke 18:15–17 and Genesis 1:26 and 2:18–23. We are all special because we are images of God. We can love and act the way God loves and acts. We can share God's life. As images of God, we want to teach others about God and his love for us. The good things we think, say, and do help others see and learn about God through us.

Vocabulary

image: the reflection of ourselves and others as in a mirror
soul: the invisible, spiritual, and immortal gift from God that gives us life

Concepts of Faith

Why are we special to God?

We are special because we are made in the image of God.

Correspondence to the *Catechism of the Catholic Church*

Man created in the image of God: *CCC* 355–57, 380–81
Equality and difference willed by God: *CCC* 369

Suggested Activity

Together look at pictures of your child as a baby. Discuss how much your child has grown.

Directions: Help the children find their way to Jesus.

Jesus said, "Let the children come to me."

Family Note

Lesson 3: I Am Special to God, Who Made Me

The two stories for this lesson are adaptations of Luke 18:15–17 and Genesis 1:26 and 2:18–23. We are all special because we are images of God. We can love and act the way God loves and acts. We can share God's life. As images of God, we want to teach others about God and his love for us. The good things we think, say, and do help others see and learn about God through us.

Vocabulary

image: the reflection of ourselves and others as in a mirror
soul: the invisible, spiritual, and immortal gift from God that gives us life

Concepts of Faith

Why are we special to God?
We are special because we are made in the image of God.

Correspondence to the *Catechism of the Catholic Church*

Man created in the image of God: *CCC* 355–57, 380–81
Equality and difference willed by God: *CCC* 369

Suggested Activity

Together look at pictures of your child as a baby. Discuss how much your child has grown.

Directions: *Find and count the things that are different. Put the number here:* __12__ .

We reflect God in different ways.

Family Note

Lesson 3: I Am Special to God, Who Made Me

The two stories for this lesson are adaptations of Luke 18:15–17 and Genesis 1:26 and 2:18–23. We are all special because we are images of God. We can love and act the way God loves and acts. We can share God's life. As images of God, we want to teach others about God and his love for us. The good things we think, say, and do help others see and learn about God through us.

Vocabulary

image: the reflection of ourselves and others as in a mirror
soul: the invisible, spiritual, and immortal gift from God that gives us life

Concepts of Faith

Why are we special to God?

We are special because we are made in the image of God.

Correspondence to the *Catechism of the Catholic Church*

Man created in the image of God: *CCC* 355–57, 380–81
Equality and difference willed by God: *CCC* 369

Suggested Activity

Together look at pictures of your child as a baby. Discuss how much your child has grown.

Directions: Circle the good actions.

Our actions should show we love God.

Family Note

Lesson 4: Actions and Attitudes—The Ten Commandments

The two stories for this lesson are adaptations of Matthew 19:16–22 and Exodus 20:1–17. God gave us the Ten Commandments to help us know how to live as his images. They are a way of life for an image of God. The Commandments are not rules or laws forced on us, but rather the way an image of God chooses to act. When we choose to act as an image of God by following the Commandments, we show our love for God.

Vocabulary

Commandments: directions God gives us so that we can know how to act as images of God
envy: unhappiness over something good that someone has

Concepts of Faith

How should we show our love for God?
We should show our love for God by choosing to follow the Commandments that he gave us.

Correspondence to the *Catechism of the Catholic Church*

The Old Law: *CCC* 1962
The Ten Commandments: *CCC* 2054–69

Suggested Activity

Work together with your child on a small project or task. Have your child help you make a cake, wash the car, set the table, make a bed, etc. Point out the steps or directions you follow to do this project or task the correct way.

Directions: Help Moses find the right way.

God gave Moses the Ten Commandments.

Family Note

Lesson 4: Actions and Attitudes—The Ten Commandments

The two stories for this lesson are adaptations of Matthew 19:16–22 and Exodus 20:1–17. God gave us the Ten Commandments to help us know how to live as his images. They are a way of life for an image of God. The Commandments are not rules or laws forced on us, but rather the way an image of God chooses to act. When we choose to act as an image of God by following the Commandments, we show our love for God.

Vocabulary

Commandments: directions God gives us so that we can know how to act as images of God
envy: unhappiness over something good that someone has

Concepts of Faith

How should we show our love for God?
We should show our love for God by choosing to follow the Commandments that he gave us.

Correspondence to the *Catechism of the Catholic Church*

The Old Law: *CCC* 1962
The Ten Commandments: *CCC* 2054–69

Suggested Activity

Work together with your child on a small project or task. Have your child help you make a cake, wash the car, set the table, make a bed, etc. Point out the steps or directions you follow to do this project or task the correct way.

Directions: Match the actions to the words.

Tell the truth.

Say your prayers.

Obey parents.

Worship God.

The Ten Commandments help us act as images of God.

Family Note

Lesson 4: Actions and Attitudes—The Ten Commandments

The two stories for this lesson are adaptations of Matthew 19:16–22 and Exodus 20:1–17. God gave us the Ten Commandments to help us know how to live as his images. They are a way of life for an image of God. The Commandments are not rules or laws forced on us, but rather the way an image of God chooses to act. When we choose to act as an image of God by following the Commandments, we show our love for God.

Vocabulary

Commandments: directions God gives us so that we can know how to act as images of God
envy: unhappiness over something good that someone has

Concepts of Faith

How should we show our love for God?
We should show our love for God by choosing to follow the Commandments that he gave us.

Correspondence to the *Catechism of the Catholic Church*

The Old Law: *CCC* 1962
The Ten Commandments: *CCC* 2054–69

Suggested Activity

Work together with your child on a small project or task. Have your child help you make a cake, wash the car, set the table, make a bed, etc. Point out the steps or directions you follow to do this project or task the correct way.

Directions: Connect the dots and finish coloring the picture.

The poor woman showed her love for God.

Family Note

Lesson 5: Love Others as God Loves You

The two stories for this lesson are adaptations of Mark 12:41–44 and Luke 10:30–37. We are made in the image of God to do what God does. God loves us; God loves everyone. Because God loves us and everyone, we should love ourselves and everyone else. First we should love God (then we should love ourselves, and then we should love others as God loves us). When we love others, we make ourselves happy because we are acting as God made us to act.

Vocabulary

love: choosing to help everyone, including ourselves, be the best images of God we can be

Concepts of Faith

Whom does God love?
God loves everyone.

Whom are we to love?
We are to love God, ourselves, and everyone else.

Correspondence to the *Catechism of the Catholic Church*

God, "He Who Is", is Truth and love: *CCC* 214, 231
God is love: *CCC* 221, 231
The Holy Spirit—God's gift: *CCC* 733
Communion in spiritual goods: *CCC* 952
Marriage in God's plan: *CCC* 1602
"Male and Female He Created Them": *CCC* 2331
Holy Orders: *CCC* 1593–98
The communal character of the human vocations: *CCC* 1878
The Christian family: *CCC* 2204–6
Conversion and society: *CCC* 1889

Suggested Activity

Give your child an extra hug. Say, "I love you."

Directions: Help the kind stranger find the man who needs help.

We should love others as God loves us.

Family Note

Lesson 5: Love Others as God Loves You

The two stories for this lesson are adaptations of Mark 12:41–44 and Luke 10:30–37. We are made in the image of God to do what God does. God loves us; God loves everyone. Because God loves us and everyone, we should love ourselves and everyone else. First we should love God (then we should love ourselves, and then we should love others as God loves us). When we love others, we make ourselves happy because we are acting as God made us to act.

Vocabulary

love: choosing to help everyone, including ourselves, be the best images of God we can be

Concepts of Faith

Whom does God love?
God loves everyone.

Whom are we to love?
We are to love God, ourselves, and everyone else.

Correspondence to the *Catechism of the Catholic Church*

God, "He Who Is", is Truth and love: *CCC* 214, 231
God is love: *CCC* 221, 231
The Holy Spirit—God's gift: *CCC* 733
Communion in spiritual goods: *CCC* 952
Marriage in God's plan: *CCC* 1602
"Male and Female He Created Them": *CCC* 2331
Holy Orders: *CCC* 1593–98
The communal character of the human vocations: *CCC* 1878
The Christian family: *CCC* 2204–6
Conversion and society: *CCC* 1889

Suggested Activity

Give your child an extra hug. Say, "I love you."

Directions: Color the pictures.

Show your love by helping others.

Family Note

Lesson 5: Love Others as God Loves You

The two stories for this lesson are adaptations of Mark 12:41–44 and Luke 10:30–37. We are made in the image of God to do what God does. God loves us; God loves everyone. Because God loves us and everyone, we should love ourselves and everyone else. First we should love God (then we should love ourselves, and then we should love others as God loves us). When we love others, we make ourselves happy because we are acting as God made us to act.

Vocabulary

love: choosing to help everyone, including ourselves, be the best images of God we can be

Concepts of Faith

Whom does God love?
God loves everyone.

Whom are we to love?
We are to love God, ourselves, and everyone else.

Correspondence to the *Catechism of the Catholic Church*

God, "He Who Is", is Truth and love: *CCC* 214, 231
God is love: *CCC* 221, 231
The Holy Spirit—God's gift: *CCC* 733
Communion in spiritual goods: *CCC* 952
Marriage in God's plan: *CCC* 1602
"Male and Female He Created Them": *CCC* 2331
Holy Orders: *CCC* 1593–98
The communal character of the human vocations: *CCC* 1878
The Christian family: *CCC* 2204–6
Conversion and society: *CCC* 1889

Suggested Activity

Give your child an extra hug. Say, "I love you."

Directions: Circle the things we see in church.

God's house is a special place.

Family Note

Lesson 6: God's House—The Church

From this lesson, the children should come to respect the items found in the church and come to know the correct behavior for church. God's house is a place of prayer and celebration. Mass is our most important prayer. At Mass, stories about God are read, and God gives us the gift of himself at Communion. Sitting quietly and listening to the stories about God, saying prayers, singing the songs, and showing respect for the things found in God's house can be gifts of love offered to God. We should be careful with the books and other things we see in church. We should remember that God is in church with us in a very special way.

Vocabulary

church: God's house on earth
pope: the man who takes Saint Peter's place and leads the whole Catholic Church on earth today
bishops: the men who today teach God's Word and help the people to be holy the way the Apostles did
priests: men who have answered God's call and have chosen to offer their lives to him and help the bishops by offering Mass and celebrating the sacraments
Bible: the book that contains the holy writings about God written by people under the guidance of the Holy Spirit
Old Testament: the first part of the Bible that tells us about God, creation, and God's love for all his people
New Testament: the second part of the Bible that tells us about Jesus, his life and Death, and the beginning of the Church

Concepts of Faith

Who serves as the leader of the whole Catholic Church on earth?
The pope.

Who are the bishops?
The bishops are men who teach God's Word and help the people to be holy the way the Apostles did.

Who are the priests?
The priests are men who have answered God's call and have chosen to offer their lives to him and help the bishops by offering Mass and celebrating the sacraments.

What is God's house on earth called?
God's house on earth is called the church.

Correspondence to the *Catechism of the Catholic Church*

Three degrees of the Sacrament of Holy Orders: *CCC* 1554–71
The Sacrament of the Eucharist: *CCC* 1324–27
What is this sacrament called?: *CCC* 1328–32
The Eucharist in the economy of salvation: *CCC* 1337–44
The movement of the celebration: *CCC* 1348–55
Names and images of the Church: *CCC* 751–52
Characteristics of the people of God: *CCC* 782
Christ is the head of this body: *CCC* 792
The Church is one, holy, Catholic, and apostolic: *CCC* 811
The Church is apostolic: *CCC* 857–60
The bishops—successors of the Apostles: *CCC* 861–63

Suggested Activity

Visit your parish church when there are no services. Let your child walk around the church looking at the statues, stained glass windows, etc.

Directions: Trace the words.

pope

bishop

priest

Family Note

Lesson 6: God's House—The Church

From this lesson, the children should come to respect the items found in the church and come to know the correct behavior for church. God's house is a place of prayer and celebration. Mass is our most important prayer. At Mass, stories about God are read, and God gives us the gift of himself at Communion. Sitting quietly and listening to the stories about God, saying prayers, singing the songs, and showing respect for the things found in God's house can be gifts of love offered to God. We should be careful with the books and other things we see in church. We should remember that God is in church with us in a very special way.

Vocabulary

church: God's house on earth

pope: the man who takes Saint Peter's place and leads the whole Catholic Church on earth today

bishops: the men who today teach God's Word and help the people to be holy the way the Apostles did

priests: men who have answered God's call and have chosen to offer their lives to him and help the bishops by offering Mass and celebrating the sacraments

Bible: the book that contains the holy writings about God written by people under the guidance of the Holy Spirit

Old Testament: the first part of the Bible that tells us about God, creation, and God's love for all his people

New Testament: the second part of the Bible that tells us about Jesus, his life and Death, and the beginning of the Church

Concepts of Faith

Who serves as the leader of the whole Catholic Church on earth?
The pope.

Who are the bishops?
The bishops are men who teach God's Word and help the people to be holy the way the Apostles did.

Who are the priests?
The priests are men who have answered God's call and have chosen to offer their lives to him and help the bishops by offering Mass and celebrating the sacraments.

What is God's house on earth called?
God's house on earth is called the church.

Correspondence to the *Catechism of the Catholic Church*

Three degrees of the Sacrament of Holy Orders: *CCC* 1554–71
The Sacrament of the Eucharist: *CCC* 1324–27
What is this sacrament called?: *CCC* 1328–32
The Eucharist in the economy of salvation: *CCC* 1337–44
The movement of the celebration: *CCC* 1348–55
Names and images of the Church: *CCC* 751–52
Characteristics of the people of God: *CCC* 782
Christ is the head of this body: *CCC* 792
The Church is one, holy, Catholic, and apostolic: *CCC* 811
The Church is apostolic: *CCC* 857–60
The bishops—successors of the Apostles: *CCC* 861–63

Suggested Activity

Visit your parish church when there are no services. Let your child walk around the church looking at the statues, stained glass windows, etc.

Directions: Count the items. Circle the correct number.

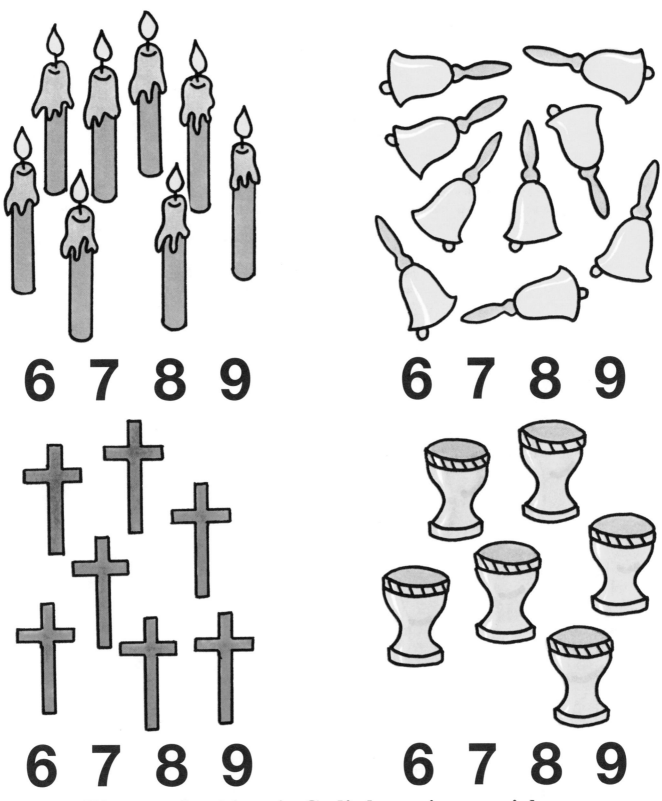

6 7 8 9

6 7 8 9

6 7 8 9

6 7 8 9

We treat the things in God's house in a special way.

Family Note

Lesson 6: God's House—The Church

From this lesson, the children should come to respect the items found in the church and come to know the correct behavior for church. God's house is a place of prayer and celebration. Mass is our most important prayer. At Mass, stories about God are read, and God gives us the gift of himself at Communion. Sitting quietly and listening to the stories about God, saying prayers, singing the songs, and showing respect for the things found in God's house can be gifts of love offered to God. We should be careful with the books and other things we see in church. We should remember that God is in church with us in a very special way.

Vocabulary

church: God's house on earth

pope: the man who takes Saint Peter's place and leads the whole Catholic Church on earth today

bishops: the men who today teach God's Word and help the people to be holy the way the Apostles did

priests: men who have answered God's call and have chosen to offer their lives to him and help the bishops by offering Mass and celebrating the sacraments

Bible: the book that contains the holy writings about God written by people under the guidance of the Holy Spirit

Old Testament: the first part of the Bible that tells us about God, creation, and God's love for all his people

New Testament: the second part of the Bible that tells us about Jesus, his life and Death, and the beginning of the Church

Concepts of Faith

Who serves as the leader of the whole Catholic Church on earth?
The pope.

Who are the bishops?
The bishops are men who teach God's Word and help the people to be holy the way the Apostles did.

Who are the priests?
The priests are men who have answered God's call and have chosen to offer their lives to him and help the bishops by offering Mass and celebrating the sacraments.

What is God's house on earth called?
God's house on earth is called the church.

Correspondence to the *Catechism of the Catholic Church*

Three degrees of the Sacrament of Holy Orders: *CCC* 1554–71
The Sacrament of the Eucharist: *CCC* 1324–27
What is this sacrament called?: *CCC* 1328–32
The Eucharist in the economy of salvation: *CCC* 1337–44
The movement of the celebration: *CCC* 1348–55
Names and images of the Church: *CCC* 751–52
Characteristics of the people of God: *CCC* 782
Christ is the head of this body: *CCC* 792
The Church is one, holy, Catholic, and apostolic: *CCC* 811
The Church is apostolic: *CCC* 857–60
The bishops—successors of the Apostles: *CCC* 861–63

Suggested Activity

Visit your parish church when there are no services. Let your child walk around the church looking at the statues, stained glass windows, etc.

Directions: Cut out the shapes. Put them where they belong.

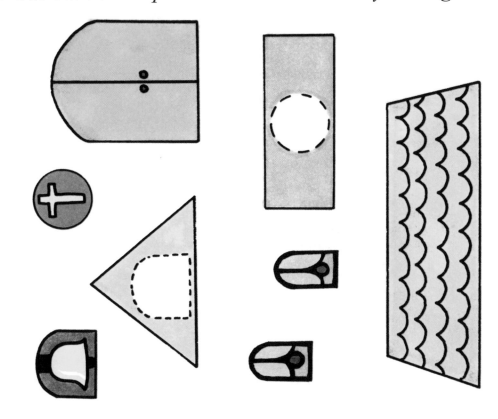

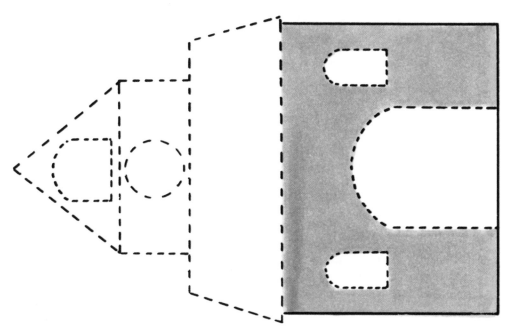

The church is God's house on earth.

Family Note

Lesson 6: God's House—The Church

From this lesson, the children should come to respect the items found in the church and come to know the correct behavior for church. God's house is a place of prayer and celebration. Mass is our most important prayer. At Mass, stories about God are read, and God gives us the gift of himself at Communion. Sitting quietly and listening to the stories about God, saying prayers, singing the songs, and showing respect for the things found in God's house can be gifts of love offered to God. We should be careful with the books and other things we see in church. We should remember that God is in church with us in a very special way.

Vocabulary

church: God's house on earth
pope: the man who takes Saint Peter's place and leads the whole Catholic Church on earth today
bishops: the men who today teach God's Word and help the people to be holy the way the Apostles did
priests: men who have answered God's call and have chosen to offer their lives to him and help the bishops by
offering Mass and celebrating the sacraments
Bible: the book that contains the holy writings about God written by people under the guidance of the Holy Spirit
Old Testament: the first part of the Bible that tells us about God, creation, and God's love for all his people
New Testament: the second part of the Bible that tells us about Jesus, his life and Death, and the beginning of
the Church

Concepts of Faith

Who serves as the leader of the whole Catholic Church on earth?
The pope.

Who are the bishops?
The bishops are men who teach God's Word and help the people to be holy the way the Apostles did.

Who are the priests?
The priests are men who have answered God's call and have chosen to offer their lives to him and help the bishops by offering Mass and celebrating the sacraments.

What is God's house on earth called?
God's house on earth is called the church.

Correspondence to the *Catechism of the Catholic Church*

Three degrees of the Sacrament of Holy Orders: *CCC* 1554–71
The Sacrament of the Eucharist: *CCC* 1324–27
What is this sacrament called?: *CCC* 1328–32
The Eucharist in the economy of salvation: *CCC* 1337–44
The movement of the celebration: *CCC* 1348–55
Names and images of the Church: *CCC* 751–52
Characteristics of the people of God: *CCC* 782
Christ is the head of this body: *CCC* 792
The Church is one, holy, Catholic, and apostolic: *CCC* 811
The Church is apostolic: *CCC* 857–60
The bishops—successors of the Apostles: *CCC* 861–63

Suggested Activity

Visit your parish church when there are no services. Let your child walk around the church looking at the statues, stained glass windows, etc.

Directions: Follow the correct path to heaven.

We can make good choices and be bright images of God.

Family Note

Lesson 7: Wrong Choices

The two stories for this lesson are adaptations of John 8:1–11 and Genesis 3:1–24. Even though most of the children are not of the age of reason and thus technically cannot sin, it is important to establish a sense of right and wrong. Along with this awareness of morality should come a sense of sorrow and a need for forgiveness when a wrong is committed. When we choose to do something we know is wrong, we are not clear images of God. We have displeased God. Sin is the opposite of love.

Vocabulary

wrong choices: choosing to do something we know is wrong, and not acting as images of God

Original Sin: the first sin of Adam and Eve and the sin we inherit from them

Concepts of Faith

What happens when we make a wrong choice?
When we make a wrong choice, we hurt ourselves, we hurt others, and we hurt God.

Correspondence to the *Catechism of the Catholic Church*

Consequences of Original Sin: *CCC* 55–58, 399–400, 402–9, 416–19
Obedience of faith: *CCC* 144–49
The Fall of man: *CCC* 385–90, 413
Man in paradise: *CCC* 374–79, 384
Original Sin: *CCC* 388–90, 396–401, 415
Reality of sin: *CCC* 386–87, 413
The spirit of the promise: *CCC* 705
Man's freedom: *CCC* 1730–42, 1743–48
Promise of a Redeemer: *CCC* 410–12, 420–21

Suggested Activity

Let your child choose an appropriate snack to make as a surprise for the rest of the family.

Directions: Circle the loving actions.

Sin is the opposite of love.

Family Note

Lesson 7: Wrong Choices

The two stories for this lesson are adaptations of John 8:1–11 and Genesis 3:1–24. Even though most of the children are not of the age of reason and thus technically cannot sin, it is important to establish a sense of right and wrong. Along with this awareness of morality should come a sense of sorrow and a need for forgiveness when a wrong is committed. When we choose to do something we know is wrong, we are not clear images of God. We have displeased God. Sin is the opposite of love.

Vocabulary

wrong choices: choosing to do something we know is wrong, and not acting as images of God

Original Sin: the first sin of Adam and Eve and the sin we inherit from them

Concepts of Faith

What happens when we make a wrong choice?
When we make a wrong choice, we hurt ourselves, we hurt others, and we hurt God.

Correspondence to the *Catechism of the Catholic Church*

Consequences of Original Sin: *CCC* 55–58, 399–400, 402–9, 416–19
Obedience of faith: *CCC* 144–49
The Fall of man: *CCC* 385–90, 413
Man in paradise: *CCC* 374–79, 384
Original Sin: *CCC* 388–90, 396–401, 415
Reality of sin: *CCC* 386–87, 413
The spirit of the promise: *CCC* 705
Man's freedom: *CCC* 1730–42, 1743–48
Promise of a Redeemer: *CCC* 410–12, 420–21

Suggested Activity

Let your child choose an appropriate snack to make as a surprise for the rest of the family.

Directions: Color the picture.

At Baptism, we become members of God's family.

Family Note

Lesson 8: God's Family—Baptism

The two stories for this lesson are adaptations of Matthew 3:1–9 and 3:13–17. Baptism is the beginning and the foundation of our union with God. Through the Sacrament of Baptism, we receive the gift of grace. Grace is God's own life. Grace makes it possible for us to act as images of God and makes us members of God's family. Therefore, grace helps us get to heaven.

Vocabulary

grace: the gift of God's life that he shares with persons
Baptism: the sacrament that takes away Original Sin and makes us members of God's family

Concepts of Faith

Who are members of God's family?
All baptized people are members of God's family.

What is grace?
Grace is the gift of God's own life that he shares with persons.

Correspondence to the *Catechism of the Catholic Church*

"In the name of the Father and of the Son and of the Holy Spirit": *CCC* 232–33
Sacraments: *CCC* 1113, 1131–34
Sacraments of Christ: *CCC* 1114–16
Sacraments of the Church: *CCC* 1117–21
Sacraments of faith: *CCC* 1122–29
Sacraments of salvation: *CCC* 1127–29
Sacraments of eternal life: *CCC* 1130
Baptism: *CCC* 1213–84

Suggested Activity

Together look at pictures from your child's Baptism. Discuss that special day.

Directions: Connect the dots. Color the picture.

The dove is a sign of the Holy Spirit.

Family Note

Lesson 8: God's Family—Baptism

The two stories for this lesson are adaptations of Matthew 3:1–9 and 3:13–17. Baptism is the beginning and the foundation of our union with God. Through the Sacrament of Baptism, we receive the gift of grace. Grace is God's own life. Grace makes it possible for us to act as images of God and makes us members of God's family. Therefore, grace helps us get to heaven.

Vocabulary

grace: the gift of God's life that he shares with persons
Baptism: the sacrament that takes away Original Sin and makes us members of God's family

Concepts of Faith

Who are members of God's family?
All baptized people are members of God's family.

What is grace?
Grace is the gift of God's own life that he shares with persons.

Correspondence to the *Catechism of the Catholic Church*

"In the name of the Father and of the Son and of the Holy Spirit": *CCC* 232–33
Sacraments: *CCC* 1113, 1131–34
Sacraments of Christ: *CCC* 1114–16
Sacraments of the Church: *CCC* 1117–21
Sacraments of faith: *CCC* 1122–29
Sacraments of salvation: *CCC* 1127–29
Sacraments of eternal life: *CCC* 1130
Baptism: *CCC* 1213–84

Suggested Activity

Together look at pictures from your child's Baptism. Discuss that special day.

Directions: *Help the prodigal son find his way home.*

We should forgive others as God forgives us.

Family Note

Lesson 9: Forgiveness Is an Act of Love

The two stories for this lesson are adaptations of Luke 15:11–32 and Matthew 18:21–35. It is important that the children understand that we all make wrong choices, sometimes causing hurt or unhappiness to others. This does not mean we are bad persons, but rather that the deed is wrong and unacceptable to God. When we have done wrong, it does not mean that God and the person we have offended no longer love us, but rather that we have hurt them and need to ask for forgiveness. We must also show through our actions that we are truly sorry and will try to do better.

Vocabulary

forgive: to put aside the hurt caused by another; to accept another's apology

Concepts of Faith

Whom do we ask to forgive us when we do something wrong?
When we do something wrong, we ask God and the person we have hurt or disobeyed to forgive us.

How should we forgive others?
We should forgive others as God forgives us.

Correspondence to the *Catechism of the Catholic Church*

The Sacrament of Penance and Reconciliation: *CCC* 1440–45, 1487
The acts of the penitent: *CCC* 1450–53
Satisfaction: *CCC* 1459

Suggested Activity

Help your child say "I'm sorry" and ask forgiveness from someone who has been offended.

Directions: Connect the dots. Color the picture.

Forgive

Forgiveness is an act of love.

Family Note

Lesson 9: Forgiveness Is an Act of Love

The two stories for this lesson are adaptations of Luke 15:11–32 and Matthew 18:21–35. It is important that the children understand that we all make wrong choices, sometimes causing hurt or unhappiness to others. This does not mean we are bad persons, but rather that the deed is wrong and unacceptable to God. When we have done wrong, it does not mean that God and the person we have offended no longer love us, but rather that we have hurt them and need to ask for forgiveness. We must also show through our actions that we are truly sorry and will try to do better.

Vocabulary

forgive: to put aside the hurt caused by another; to accept another's apology

Concepts of Faith

Whom do we ask to forgive us when we do something wrong?
When we do something wrong, we ask God and the person we have hurt or disobeyed to forgive us.

How should we forgive others?
We should forgive others as God forgives us.

Correspondence to the *Catechism of the Catholic Church*

The Sacrament of Penance and Reconciliation: *CCC* 1440–45, 1487
The acts of the penitent: *CCC* 1450–53
Satisfaction: *CCC* 1459

Suggested Activity

Help your child say "I'm sorry" and ask forgiveness from someone who has been offended.

Directions: Color the good actions.

Forgive others as God forgives you.

Family Note

Lesson 9: Forgiveness Is an Act of Love

The two stories for this lesson are adaptations of Luke 15:11–32 and Matthew 18:21–35. It is important that the children understand that we all make wrong choices, sometimes causing hurt or unhappiness to others. This does not mean we are bad persons, but rather that the deed is wrong and unacceptable to God. When we have done wrong, it does not mean that God and the person we have offended no longer love us, but rather that we have hurt them and need to ask for forgiveness. We must also show through our actions that we are truly sorry and will try to do better.

Vocabulary

forgive: to put aside the hurt caused by another; to accept another's apology

Concepts of Faith

Whom do we ask to forgive us when we do something wrong?
When we do something wrong, we ask God and the person we have hurt or disobeyed to forgive us.

How should we forgive others?
We should forgive others as God forgives us.

Correspondence to the *Catechism of the Catholic Church*

The Sacrament of Penance and Reconciliation: *CCC* 1440–45, 1487
The acts of the penitent: *CCC* 1450–53
Satisfaction: *CCC* 1459

Suggested Activity

Help your child say "I'm sorry" and ask forgiveness from someone who has been offended.

Our Father Booklet

hallowed be thy name.

GOD

God's name is holy.

Our Father, who art in heaven,

God, our Father, is in heaven.

Family Note

Lesson 10: Prayer

The two stories for this lesson are adaptations of Luke 11:1–4 and 18:9–14. The Our Father is introduced in this lesson. Jesus prayed often and taught others how to pray. Jesus wants us to follow his example and pray often to our Father in heaven. God hears all our prayers even when we do not say the words out loud. Sometimes we do not get what we pray for because God knows what is best for us.

Vocabulary

prayer: raising our hearts and minds to God by talking to him
hallowed: holy
trespasses: wrong choices against someone
temptation: something that makes a wrong choice look good

Concepts of Faith

What is prayer?

Prayer is raising our hearts and minds to God by talking with him. We can pray quietly or out loud, alone or with others. We can say "thank you", ask for help, say "I'm sorry", adore God, and sing God's praises.

Correspondence to the *Catechism of the Catholic Church*

Prayer as God's gift: *CCC* 2559–65, 2590, 2644
In the fullness of time: *CCC* 2598–606, 2620
Jesus teaches how to pray: *CCC* 2607–15, 2621
Jesus hears our prayers: *CCC* 2616, 2621
Blessing and adoration: *CCC* 2626–28, 2645
Prayer of petition: *CCC* 2629–33, 2646
Prayers of intercession: *CCC* 2634–36, 2647
Prayer of thanksgiving: *CCC* 2637–38, 2648
Prayers of praise: *CCC* 2639–43, 2649
Prayer to the Father: *CCC* 2664, 2680
Prayer to Jesus: *CCC* 2665–69, 2680
"Come, Holy Spirit": *CCC* 2670–72, 2681
In communion with the holy Mother of God: *CCC* 2673–79, 2682
A cloud of witnesses: *CCC* 2683–84, 2692
Places favorable for prayer: *CCC* 2691, 2696
Filial trust: *CCC* 2734–41, 2756
"The summary of the whole gospel": *CCC* 2761–76
The seven petitions: *CCC* 2803–6, 2857
"We Dare to Say": *CCC* 2777–96, 2797–802
"Hallowed Be Thy Name": *CCC* 2807–15, 2858
"Thy Kingdom Come": *CCC* 2816–21, 2859
"Thy Will Be Done on Earth as It Is in Heaven": *CCC* 2822–27, 2860
"Give Us This Day Our Daily Bread": *CCC* 2828–37, 2861
"Forgive Us Our Trespasses, as We Forgive Those Who Trespass Against Us": *CCC* 2838–45, 2862
"And Lead Us Not into Temptation": *CCC* 2846–49, 2863
"But Deliver Us from Evil": *CCC* 2850–54, 2864
The final doxology: *CCC* 2855–56, 2865

Suggested Activity

Review the Our Father with your child.

Our Father Booklet

Give us this day our daily bread,

Give us what we need to live now and later with you in heaven.

Thy kingdom come. Thy will be done on earth, as it is in heaven.

We will try to live as images of God on earth.

Our Father Booklet

and lead us not into temptation, but deliver us from evil. Amen.

Help us make good choices and keep us safe in your love.

and forgive us our trespasses as we forgive those who trespass against us,

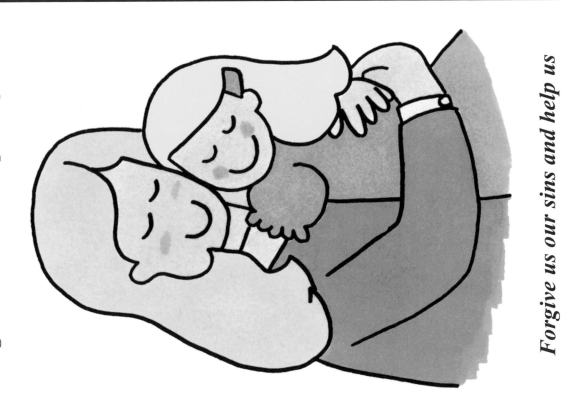

Forgive us our sins and help us forgive others.

Directions: Color by number.

Blue **1**   Pink **2**   Green **3**   Yellow **4**   Orange **5**

The Bible helps us learn about God, our Father.

Family Note

Lesson 10: Prayer

The two stories for this lesson are adaptations of Luke 11:1–4 and 18:9–14. The Our Father is introduced in this lesson. Jesus prayed often and taught others how to pray. Jesus wants us to follow his example and pray often to our Father in heaven. God hears all our prayers even when we do not say the words out loud. Sometimes we do not get what we pray for because God knows what is best for us.

Vocabulary

prayer: raising our hearts and minds to God by talking to him
hallowed: holy
trespasses: wrong choices against someone
temptation: something that makes a wrong choice look good

Concepts of Faith

What is prayer?

Prayer is raising our hearts and minds to God by talking with him. We can pray quietly or out loud, alone or with others. We can say "thank you", ask for help, say "I'm sorry", adore God, and sing God's praises.

Correspondence to the *Catechism of the Catholic Church*

Prayer as God's gift: *CCC* 2559–65, 2590, 2644
In the fullness of time: *CCC* 2598–606, 2620
Jesus teaches how to pray: *CCC* 2607–15, 2621
Jesus hears our prayers: *CCC* 2616, 2621
Blessing and adoration: *CCC* 2626–28, 2645
Prayer of petition: *CCC* 2629–33, 2646
Prayers of intercession: *CCC* 2634–36, 2647
Prayer of thanksgiving: *CCC* 2637–38, 2648
Prayers of praise: *CCC* 2639–43, 2649
Prayer to the Father: *CCC* 2664, 2680
Prayer to Jesus: *CCC* 2665–69, 2680
"Come, Holy Spirit": *CCC* 2670–72, 2681
In communion with the holy Mother of God: *CCC* 2673–79, 2682
A cloud of witnesses: *CCC* 2683–84, 2692
Places favorable for prayer: *CCC* 2691, 2696
Filial trust: *CCC* 2734–41, 2756
"The summary of the whole gospel": *CCC* 2761–76
The seven petitions: *CCC* 2803–6, 2857
"We Dare to Say": *CCC* 2777–96, 2797–802
"Hallowed Be Thy Name": *CCC* 2807–15, 2858
"Thy Kingdom Come": *CCC* 2816–21, 2859
"Thy Will Be Done on Earth as It Is in Heaven": *CCC* 2822–27, 2860
"Give Us This Day Our Daily Bread": *CCC* 2828–37, 2861
"Forgive Us Our Trespasses, as We Forgive Those Who Trespass Against Us": *CCC* 2838–45, 2862
"And Lead Us Not into Temptation": *CCC* 2846–49, 2863
"But Deliver Us from Evil": *CCC* 2850–54, 2864
The final doxology: *CCC* 2855–56, 2865

Suggested Activity

Review the Our Father with your child.

Directions: Circle the actions of prayer.

God hears all our prayers.

Family Note

Lesson 10: Prayer

The two stories for this lesson are adaptations of Luke 11:1–4 and 18:9–14. The Our Father is introduced in this lesson. Jesus prayed often and taught others how to pray. Jesus wants us to follow his example and pray often to our Father in heaven. God hears all our prayers even when we do not say the words out loud. Sometimes we do not get what we pray for because God knows what is best for us.

Vocabulary

prayer: raising our hearts and minds to God by talking to him
hallowed: holy
trespasses: wrong choices against someone
temptation: something that makes a wrong choice look good

Concepts of Faith

What is prayer?

Prayer is raising our hearts and minds to God by talking with him. We can pray quietly or out loud, alone or with others. We can say "thank you", ask for help, say "I'm sorry", adore God, and sing God's praises.

Correspondence to the *Catechism of the Catholic Church*

Prayer as God's gift: *CCC* 2559–65, 2590, 2644
In the fullness of time: *CCC* 2598–606, 2620
Jesus teaches how to pray: *CCC* 2607–15, 2621
Jesus hears our prayers: *CCC* 2616, 2621
Blessing and adoration: *CCC* 2626–28, 2645
Prayer of petition: *CCC* 2629–33, 2646
Prayers of intercession: *CCC* 2634–36, 2647
Prayer of thanksgiving: *CCC* 2637–38, 2648
Prayers of praise: *CCC* 2639–43, 2649
Prayer to the Father: *CCC* 2664, 2680
Prayer to Jesus: *CCC* 2665–69, 2680
"Come, Holy Spirit": *CCC* 2670–72, 2681
In communion with the holy Mother of God: *CCC* 2673–79, 2682
A cloud of witnesses: *CCC* 2683–84, 2692
Places favorable for prayer: *CCC* 2691, 2696
Filial trust: *CCC* 2734–41, 2756
"The summary of the whole gospel": *CCC* 2761–76
The seven petitions: *CCC* 2803–6, 2857
"We Dare to Say": *CCC* 2777–96, 2797–802
"Hallowed Be Thy Name": *CCC* 2807–15, 2858
"Thy Kingdom Come": *CCC* 2816–21, 2859
"Thy Will Be Done on Earth as It Is in Heaven": *CCC* 2822–27, 2860
"Give Us This Day Our Daily Bread": *CCC* 2828–37, 2861
"Forgive Us Our Trespasses, as We Forgive Those Who Trespass Against Us": *CCC* 2838–45, 2862
"And Lead Us Not into Temptation": *CCC* 2846–49, 2863
"But Deliver Us from Evil": *CCC* 2850–54, 2864
The final doxology: *CCC* 2855–56, 2865

Suggested Activity

Review the Our Father with your child.

Directions: *Color the small beads yellow.*
Color the big beads purple.

Yellow

Purple

When we pray the Rosary, we think about Jesus' life.

Family Note

Lesson 11: The Rosary

This lesson is an introduction to the Rosary. When we say the Rosary, we think about the special events in Jesus' life. We pray the joyful, sorrowful, and glorious mysteries. The rosary beads help us count the number of prayers that we have said. When we pray the Rosary, we ask Mary to ask Jesus to keep us in his loving care.

Vocabulary

Rosary: a special prayer in honor of the Blessed Virgin Mary that helps us remember and think about special events in the lives of Jesus and Mary

Concepts of Faith

What does the Rosary help us remember?

The Rosary helps us remember and think about special events in the lives of Jesus and Mary.

Correspondence to the *Catechism of the Catholic Church*

Prayer of the Virgin Mary: *CCC* 2617–19, 2622

Suggested Activity

Show your child the rosary you use. Review the prayers of the Rosary that your child knows: the Our Father, the Hail Mary, and the Glory Be.

Mass Booklet

The priest reads a story about Jesus' life on earth.

The priest and the altar boys walk to the altar.

Family Note

Lesson 12: Mass

The story for this lesson is an adaptation of Luke 24:13–35. In this lesson, the children are introduced to the Mass as the most perfect form of prayer. The Mass is offered to God to worship him, to thank him, to say we are sorry for our sins, and to ask for help. It is the sacrifice of Jesus on the Cross, offered in our church by the priests. As the family of God, we listen carefully at Mass, say the prayers, and sing the songs.

Vocabulary

Mass: the Mass makes present Jesus' sacrifice of love—his Death on the Cross under the appearance of bread and wine. At the Mass we can receive Holy Communion.

Consecration: the most important part of the Mass, when the bread and wine are changed into the Body and Blood of Jesus. Jesus is present and living, whole and entire, both under the appearances of bread and wine.

Holy Communion: Jesus received by people under the appearances of bread and wine

Concepts of Faith

What is Mass?
The Mass makes present Jesus' sacrifice of love—his Death on the Cross—under the appearances of bread and wine. At Mass, we can receive Holy Communion.

What happens at Mass?
At Mass, stories about God are read, and bread and wine are changed into Jesus' Body and Blood, through which God gives us the gift of himself at Communion. At Mass, we love Jesus, and Jesus loves us just as he did when he gave his life on the Cross.

When was the first Mass?
Jesus offered the first Mass at the Last Supper.

Correspondence to the *Catechism of the Catholic Church*

The institution of the Eucharist: *CCC* 1337–340
"Do this in memory of me": *CCC* 1341–344
The movement of the celebration: *CCC* 1348–355
The sacrificial memorial of Christ and of his Body, the Church: *CCC* 1366
The Paschal Banquet: *CCC* 1382–390

Suggested Activity

Have your child attend Mass with you. Sit near the front and help your child follow the Mass using the Mass booklet made in school.

Mass Booklet

The priest says, "This is My Body."

We should offer ourselves in love as a gift to God.

Mass Booklet

We offer each other a sign of peace.

The Consecration is the most important part of the Mass.

Mass Booklet

The priest blesses us as he makes the Sign of the Cross.

We receive Jesus in a special way.

Directions: Trace the letters.

Family Note

Lesson 13: Jesus Is God the Son

The two stories for this lesson are adaptations of Luke 4:14–30 and John 4:4–30. Jesus is God the Son, the second person of the Blessed Trinity. Jesus is the one whose coming was foretold in the Scriptures. He came down from heaven to save us from our sins—that is, to redeem us. Thus, he shows us who we are and makes it possible for us to live as images of God now and to be happy forever with God in heaven.

Vocabulary

scroll: roll of paper with writing on it—the first books

Bible: the book that contains the holy writings about God written by people under the guidance of the Holy Spirit

Old Testament: the first part of the Bible that tells us about God, creation, and God's love for all his people

New Testament: the second part of the Bible that tells us about Jesus, his life and Death, and the beginning of the Church

Concepts of Faith

Who is Jesus?

Jesus is God the Son, the second person of the Blessed Trinity, who became man.

Correspondence to the *Catechism of the Catholic Church*

Jesus: *CCC* 430–35

The only Son of God: *CCC* 441–45, 454

The Son of God became man: *CCC* 456–63

Suggested Activity

Show your child your family Bible or a Bible you use.

Directions: Connect the dots.

The woman found something much better than water.

Family Note

Lesson 13: Jesus Is God the Son

The two stories for this lesson are adaptations of Luke 4:14–30 and John 4:4–30. Jesus is God the Son, the second person of the Blessed Trinity. Jesus is the one whose coming was foretold in the Scriptures. He came down from heaven to save us from our sins—that is, to redeem us. Thus, he shows us who we are and makes it possible for us to live as images of God now and to be happy forever with God in heaven.

Vocabulary

scroll: roll of paper with writing on it—the first books

Bible: the book that contains the holy writings about God written by people under the guidance of the Holy Spirit

Old Testament: the first part of the Bible that tells us about God, creation, and God's love for all his people

New Testament: the second part of the Bible that tells us about Jesus, his life and Death, and the beginning of the Church

Concepts of Faith

Who is Jesus?

Jesus is God the Son, the second person of the Blessed Trinity, who became man.

Correspondence to the *Catechism of the Catholic Church*

Jesus: *CCC* 430–35

The only Son of God: *CCC* 441–45, 454

The Son of God became man: *CCC* 456–63

Suggested Activity

Show your child your family Bible or a Bible you use.

Directions: Match what Jesus had to what we have today.

Jesus lived on earth long ago. Jesus is God the Son.

Family Note

Lesson 13: Jesus Is God the Son

The two stories for this lesson are adaptations of Luke 4:14–30 and John 4:4–30. Jesus is God the Son, the second person of the Blessed Trinity. Jesus is the one whose coming was foretold in the Scriptures. He came down from heaven to save us from our sins—that is, to redeem us. Thus, he shows us who we are and makes it possible for us to live as images of God now and to be happy forever with God in heaven.

Vocabulary

scroll: roll of paper with writing on it—the first books
Bible: the book that contains the holy writings about God written by people under the guidance of the Holy Spirit
Old Testament: the first part of the Bible that tells us about God, creation, and God's love for all his people
New Testament: the second part of the Bible that tells us about Jesus, his life and Death, and the beginning of the Church

Concepts of Faith

Who is Jesus?

Jesus is God the Son, the second person of the Blessed Trinity, who became man.

Correspondence to the *Catechism of the Catholic Church*

Jesus: *CCC* 430–35
The only Son of God: *CCC* 441–45, 454
The Son of God became man: *CCC* 456–63

Suggested Activity

Show your child your family Bible or a Bible you use.

Directions: Find and color the hidden water jugs.

Jesus changed the water into wine.

Family Note

Lesson 14: Miracles of Jesus

The two stories for this lesson are adaptations of John 2:1–11 and 6:4–30. The miracles that Jesus performed were not done by magic tricks. Jesus really did heal the sick, change water into wine, multiply the loaves and fishes. He could perform miracles because he is God the Son. The miracles Jesus worked helped people believe in what he said. As images of God, we can help others believe in and follow Jesus.

Vocabulary

miracle: something that can be done only by the power of God

Concepts of Faith

Who is Jesus?
Jesus is God the Son, the second person of the Blessed Trinity, who became man.

How are miracles performed?
Miracles are performed through the power of God.

Correspondence to the *Catechism of the Catholic Church*

The signs of the kingdom of God: *CCC* 547–50

Suggested Activity

You and your child may work together to do something nice for another member of your family. Talk about how Jesus helped others.

Directions: Cut out the loaves and fishes. Glue them in the basket.

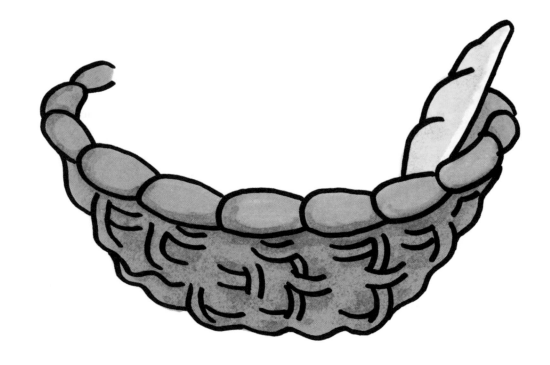

Jesus can do miracles because he is God the Son.

Family Note

Lesson 14: Miracles of Jesus

The two stories for this lesson are adaptations of John 2:1–11 and 6:4–30. The miracles that Jesus performed were not done by magic tricks. Jesus really did heal the sick, change water into wine, multiply the loaves and fishes. He could perform miracles because he is God the Son. The miracles Jesus worked helped people believe in what he said. As images of God, we can help others believe in and follow Jesus.

Vocabulary

miracle: something that can be done only by the power of God

Concepts of Faith

Who is Jesus?
Jesus is God the Son, the second person of the Blessed Trinity, who became man.

How are miracles performed?
Miracles are performed through the power of God.

Correspondence to the *Catechism of the Catholic Church*

The signs of the kingdom of God: *CCC 547–50*

Suggested Activity

You and your child may work together to do something nice for another member of your family. Talk about how Jesus helped others.

Directions: Circle the miracles.

Jesus did not do magic. Jesus worked miracles.

Family Note

Lesson 14: Miracles of Jesus

The two stories for this lesson are adaptations of John 2:1–11 and 6:4–30. The miracles that Jesus performed were not done by magic tricks. Jesus really did heal the sick, change water into wine, multiply the loaves and fishes. He could perform miracles because he is God the Son. The miracles Jesus worked helped people believe in what he said. As images of God, we can help others believe in and follow Jesus.

Vocabulary

miracle: something that can be done only by the power of God

Concepts of Faith

Who is Jesus?
Jesus is God the Son, the second person of the Blessed Trinity, who became man.

How are miracles performed?
Miracles are performed through the power of God.

Correspondence to the *Catechism of the Catholic Church*

The signs of the kingdom of God: *CCC* 547–50

Suggested Activity

You and your child may work together to do something nice for another member of your family. Talk about how Jesus helped others.

Directions: Trace each fishing line to the fish.

Jesus said, "Come follow me."

Family Note

Lesson 15: Jesus Says, "Come Follow Me"

The two stories for this lesson are adaptations of Luke 5:1–11 and Matthew 4:18–22. Jesus extended the invitation to follow him repeatedly throughout his life on earth. He extended the invitation to follow him (to do as he did) to the Apostles. They answered Jesus' call and chose to follow him and to lead others to him. Jesus asks all people to follow him. We follow Jesus by being the best images of God we can be.

Vocabulary

Apostles: twelve friends called by Jesus to follow him. They answered Jesus' call and were sent by him to teach others about him and do his work in a special way.

Gospels: the four books of the New Testament that tell of the life, Death, and Resurrection of Jesus

Concepts of Faith

Who were the Apostles?

The Apostles were twelve friends called by Jesus to follow him. They answered Jesus' call and were sent by him to teach others about him and to do his work in a special way.

Who were the four followers of Jesus' who wrote the Gospels?

Matthew, Mark, Luke, and John.

Correspondence to the *Catechism of the Catholic Church*

The Church is apostolic: *CCC* 857
The Apostles' mission: *CCC* 858–60
The bishops—successors of the Apostles: *CCC* 861–62

Suggested Activity

Play "follow the leader" with your child.

Directions: Find and color the hidden fish.

Jesus filled the fishermen's nets.

Family Note

Lesson 15: Jesus Says, "Come Follow Me"

The two stories for this lesson are adaptations of Luke 5:1–11 and Matthew 4:18–22. Jesus extended the invitation to follow him repeatedly throughout his life on earth. He extended the invitation to follow him (to do as he did) to the Apostles. They answered Jesus' call and chose to follow him and to lead others to him. Jesus asks all people to follow him. We follow Jesus by being the best images of God we can be.

Vocabulary

Apostles: twelve friends called by Jesus to follow him. They answered Jesus' call and were sent by him to teach others about him and do his work in a special way.

Gospels: the four books of the New Testament that tell of the life, Death, and Resurrection of Jesus

Concepts of Faith

Who were the Apostles?
The Apostles were twelve friends called by Jesus to follow him. They answered Jesus' call and were sent by him to teach others about him and to do his work in a special way.

Who were the four followers of Jesus' who wrote the Gospels?
Matthew, Mark, Luke, and John.

Correspondence to the *Catechism of the Catholic Church*

The Church is apostolic: *CCC* 857
The Apostles' mission: *CCC* 858–60
The bishops—successors of the Apostles: *CCC* 861–62

Suggested Activity

Play "follow the leader" with your child.

Directions: Count the fish. Write the correct number.

Jesus said, "I will make you fishers of men."

Family Note

Lesson 15: Jesus Says, "Come Follow Me"

The two stories for this lesson are adaptations of Luke 5:1–11 and Matthew 4:18–22. Jesus extended the invitation to follow him repeatedly throughout his life on earth. He extended the invitation to follow him (to do as he did) to the Apostles. They answered Jesus' call and chose to follow him and to lead others to him. Jesus asks all people to follow him. We follow Jesus by being the best images of God we can be.

Vocabulary

Apostles: twelve friends called by Jesus to follow him. They answered Jesus' call and were sent by him to teach others about him and do his work in a special way.

Gospels: the four books of the New Testament that tell of the life, Death, and Resurrection of Jesus

Concepts of Faith

Who were the Apostles?
The Apostles were twelve friends called by Jesus to follow him. They answered Jesus' call and were sent by him to teach others about him and to do his work in a special way.

Who were the four followers of Jesus' who wrote the Gospels?
Matthew, Mark, Luke, and John.

Correspondence to the *Catechism of the Catholic Church*

The Church is apostolic: *CCC* 857
The Apostles' mission: *CCC* 858–60
The bishops—successors of the Apostles: *CCC* 861–62

Suggested Activity

Play "follow the leader" with your child.

Directions: Circle the actions that draw us closer to God.

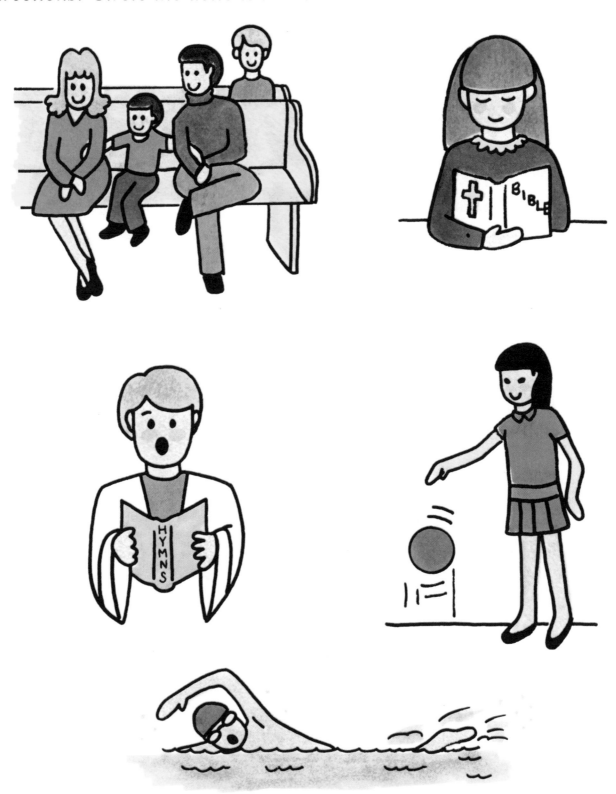

Jesus is our example. He shows us how to live.

Family Note

Lesson 16: Jesus, Our Example

This lesson is an introduction to the corporal works of mercy. We introduce them as the good works we can do to follow Jesus' example. Jesus is our perfect example. He shows us God and therefore how we should live as images of God. Everything we experience, except sin, he experienced. In Christ, by the power of the Holy Spirit, every human activity, except sin, is raised to the level of the divine.

Vocabulary

example: someone or something that shows us how something is done
soul: the invisible, spiritual, and immortal gift from God that gives us life
saints: holy men and women who followed Jesus and now live with God in heaven

Concepts of Faith

Who is our perfect example?
Jesus is our perfect example.

How do we follow Jesus' example?
We follow Jesus' example by doing what Jesus did.

Correspondence to the *Catechism of the Catholic Church*

Body and soul but truly one: *CCC* 362–66
Why did the Word become flesh?: *CCC* 457–60
Love for the poor: *CCC* 2443–47

Suggested Activity

Together with your child, help an elderly neighbor, parishioner, or relative complete his yard work or do a household chore.

Directions: Follow the lighted candles to heaven.

Start here →

Jesus is the light of our lives.

Family Note

Lesson 16: Jesus, Our Example

This lesson is an introduction to the corporal works of mercy. We introduce them as the good works we can do to follow Jesus' example. Jesus is our perfect example. He shows us God and therefore how we should live as images of God. Everything we experience, except sin, he experienced. In Christ, by the power of the Holy Spirit, every human activity, except sin, is raised to the level of the divine.

Vocabulary

example: someone or something that shows us how something is done
soul: the invisible, spiritual, and immortal gift from God that gives us life
saints: holy men and women who followed Jesus and now live with God in heaven

Concepts of Faith

Who is our perfect example?
Jesus is our perfect example.

How do we follow Jesus' example?
We follow Jesus' example by doing what Jesus did.

Correspondence to the *Catechism of the Catholic Church*

Body and soul but truly one: *CCC* 362–66
Why did the Word become flesh?: *CCC* 457–60
Love for the poor: *CCC* 2443–47

Suggested Activity

Together with your child, help an elderly neighbor, parishioner, or relative complete his yard work or do a household chore.

Directions: Match the pictures to the words.

Jesus is God the Son.

The dove is a sign of the Holy Spirit.

The church is God's house on earth.

There are three persons in one God.

We have faith in God. We believe in him.

Family Note

Lesson 17: Faith and Trust

The two stories for this lesson are adaptations of Luke 8:22–25 and Genesis 6:14–22, 8:6–12, and 9:8–17. God made us to do good things. When we live good lives, we are showing our faith and saying "Yes" to God. Jesus, God the Son, teaches us what are truly good actions. By following Jesus' example and the teachings of his Church, we practice our faith and show God our love.

Vocabulary

faith: the gift that God gives us that helps us to believe in him and all he has taught
trust: knowing that you will be safe with someone because that person loves you and only wants good things for you

Concepts of Faith

What is faith?
Faith is the gift that God gives us that helps us to believe in him and all he has taught.

Correspondence to the *Catechism of the Catholic Church*

Faith: *CCC* 26, 142, 150, 153, 1814, 2087
Trust: *CCC* 301, 304, 2115, 2547, 2828, 2836, 2861

Suggested Activity

Read a Bible story to your child.

Directions: Cut out the puzzle pieces. Put the puzzle together.

Family Note

Lesson 17: Faith and Trust

The two stories for this lesson are adaptations of Luke 8:22–25 and Genesis 6:14–22, 8:6–12, and 9:8–17. God made us to do good things. When we live good lives, we are showing our faith and saying "Yes" to God. Jesus, God the Son, teaches us what are truly good actions. By following Jesus' example and the teachings of his Church, we practice our faith and show God our love.

Vocabulary

faith: the gift that God gives us that helps us to believe in him and all he has taught
trust: knowing that you will be safe with someone because that person loves you and only wants good things for you

Concepts of Faith

What is faith?
Faith is the gift that God gives us that helps us to believe in him and all he has taught.

Correspondence to the *Catechism of the Catholic Church*

Faith: *CCC* 26, 142, 150, 153, 1814, 2087
Trust: *CCC* 301, 304, 2115, 2547, 2828, 2836, 2861

Suggested Activity

Read a Bible story to your child.

Directions: Lead the animals to the ark.

God said, "Take two of every creature onto the ark."

Family Note

Lesson 17: Faith and Trust

The two stories for this lesson are adaptations of Luke 8:22–25 and Genesis 6:14–22, 8:6–12, and 9:8–17. God made us to do good things. When we live good lives, we are showing our faith and saying "Yes" to God. Jesus, God the Son, teaches us what are truly good actions. By following Jesus' example and the teachings of his Church, we practice our faith and show God our love.

Vocabulary

faith: the gift that God gives us that helps us to believe in him and all he has taught
trust: knowing that you will be safe with someone because that person loves you and only wants good things for you

Concepts of Faith

What is faith?
Faith is the gift that God gives us that helps us to believe in him and all he has taught.

Correspondence to the *Catechism of the Catholic Church*

Faith: *CCC* 26, 142, 150, 153, 1814, 2087
Trust: *CCC* 301, 304, 2115, 2547, 2828, 2836, 2861

Suggested Activity

Read a Bible story to your child.

Directions: Color the butterfly.

A butterfly is a sign of new life.

Family Note

Lesson 18: After Death There Is Life

The two stories for this lesson are adaptations of John 11:17–44 and Mark 5:21–24, 35–43. When someone dies, that person's life does not end; it changes. When people die, they begin new lives with God in heaven, if they have followed Jesus' example. We are still images of God even after we have died. We pray for all those who have died so they may receive new life with God in heaven.

Vocabulary

death: the end of a person's life on earth and the beginning of his everlasting life
soul: the invisible gift from God that gives us life and lives forever
grave: a place where the body of someone who died is buried

Concepts of Faith

Is dying the end of our lives?

No, if we have lived as images of God then it is the beginning of new life with God in heaven.

Correspondence to the *Catechism of the Catholic Church*

"I believe in the resurrection of the body": *CCC* 988–91, 1015–19
Christ's Resurrection and ours: *CCC* 992–1004
Dying in Christ Jesus: *CCC* 1005–14

Suggested Activity

Tell your child about a relative or friend who has died. Say a prayer with your child for that person.

Directions: Which happened first, second, and third? Write the correct numbers in the boxes.

We thank God for the gift of new life.

Family Note

Lesson 18: After Death There Is Life

The two stories for this lesson are adaptations of John 11:17–44 and Mark 5:21–24, 35–43. When someone dies, that person's life does not end; it changes. When people die, they begin new lives with God in heaven, if they have followed Jesus' example. We are still images of God even after we have died. We pray for all those who have died so they may receive new life with God in heaven.

Vocabulary

death: the end of a person's life on earth and the beginning of his everlasting life
soul: the invisible gift from God that gives us life and lives forever
grave: a place where the body of someone who died is buried

Concepts of Faith

Is dying the end of our lives?

No, if we have lived as images of God then it is the beginning of new life with God in heaven.

Correspondence to the *Catechism of the Catholic Church*

"I believe in the resurrection of the body": *CCC* 988–91, 1015–19
Christ's Resurrection and ours: *CCC* 992–1004
Dying in Christ Jesus: *CCC* 1005–14

Suggested Activity

Tell your child about a relative or friend who has died. Say a prayer with your child for that person.

Directions: Cut out the pictures. Put them in the correct order.

Family Note

Lesson 18: After Death There Is Life

The two stories for this lesson are adaptations of John 11:17–44 and Mark 5:21–24, 35–43. When someone dies, that person's life does not end; it changes. When people die, they begin new lives with God in heaven, if they have followed Jesus' example. We are still images of God even after we have died. We pray for all those who have died so they may receive new life with God in heaven.

Vocabulary

death: the end of a person's life on earth and the beginning of his everlasting life
soul: the invisible gift from God that gives us life and lives forever
grave: a place where the body of someone who died is buried

Concepts of Faith

Is dying the end of our lives?
No, if we have lived as images of God then it is the beginning of new life with God in heaven.

Correspondence to the *Catechism of the Catholic Church*

"I believe in the resurrection of the body": *CCC* 988–91, 1015–19
Christ's Resurrection and ours: *CCC* 992–1004
Dying in Christ Jesus: *CCC* 1005–14

Suggested Activity

Tell your child about a relative or friend who has died. Say a prayer with your child for that person.

Directions: Match the people to the places they each teach us about God.

Family Note

Lesson 19: God Should Come First in Our Lives

The two stories for this lesson are adaptations of Luke 4:1–13 and Matthew 7:24–29. When we live our lives showing that we are images of God in all we think, say, and do, then we show that God comes first for us. It may not always be easy to do what is right, but when we obey and think of others before ourselves, we are living as Jesus taught and showing that God is most important in our lives. The material things we have—toys, jewelry, houses, money, etc.—are good and are for our use, but they are not the most important part of our lives. God should be first in our lives.

Vocabulary

tempt: to make a wrong choice look good
parable: a story Jesus told to teach about God, heaven, and how we are to act

Concepts of Faith

Who is most important in our lives?
God is most important in our lives.

How do we show God is most important?
We show that God is most important by acting as images of God in all we think, say, and do.

Correspondence to the *Catechism of the Catholic Church*

Heaven: *CCC* 1023–29, 1052–53
Jesus teaches how to pray: *CCC* 2607–15, 2621
New law or law of the Gospel: *CCC* 1965–74, 1977, 1983–86
What is prayer?: *CCC* 2559–65, 2590, 2644

Suggested Activity

Have your child gather some outgrown toys or clothes to give to the needy.

Directions: Cut out the house. Glue the house on the rock.

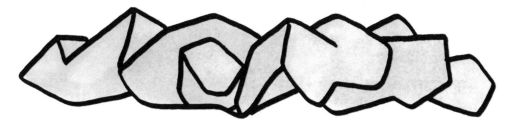

**The wise man built his house on the rock.
We should build our lives with God.**

Family Note

Lesson 19: God Should Come First in Our Lives

The two stories for this lesson are adaptations of Luke 4:1–13 and Matthew 7:24–29. When we live our lives showing that we are images of God in all we think, say, and do, then we show that God comes first for us. It may not always be easy to do what is right, but when we obey and think of others before ourselves, we are living as Jesus taught and showing that God is most important in our lives. The material things we have—toys, jewelry, houses, money, etc.—are good and are for our use, but they are not the most important part of our lives. God should be first in our lives.

Vocabulary

tempt: to make a wrong choice look good
parable: a story Jesus told to teach about God, heaven, and how we are to act

Concepts of Faith

Who is most important in our lives?
God is most important in our lives.

How do we show God is most important?
We show that God is most important by acting as images of God in all we think, say, and do.

Correspondence to the *Catechism of the Catholic Church*

Heaven: *CCC* 1023–29, 1052–53
Jesus teaches how to pray: *CCC* 2607–15, 2621
New law or law of the Gospel: *CCC* 1965–74, 1977, 1983–86
What is prayer?: *CCC* 2559–65, 2590, 2644

Suggested Activity

Have your child gather some outgrown toys or clothes to give to the needy.

Directions: *Color the bird with the longest legs blue.*
Color the smallest bird yellow.
Color the bird with the biggest tail red.

God cares for all that he has made.

Family Note

Lesson 20: God Cares for Us and All He Has Made

The two stories for this lesson are adaptations of Matthew 6:26–34 and 18:10–14, and John 10:11–15. God is the source of all we have and all we need. He loves us. He wants to share his life with us now and he wants us to be with him someday in heaven. God has told us, shown us, and given us all that we need to be the best images of God we can be. Jesus told us that God takes care of all that he has made. We know God loves and takes care of us.

Vocabulary

Divine Providence: God's all-wise plan for all he has created and his loving care for all creation

Concepts of Faith

Who takes care of us always?
God takes care of us always.

Correspondence to the *Catechism of the Catholic Church*

God carries out his plan—divine providence: *CCC* 302–5, 320–23

Suggested Activity

Review the Guardian Angel Prayer with your child:

Angel of God,
my guardian dear,
to whom God's love commits me here,
ever this day be at my side,
to light and guard, to rule and guide.
Amen.

Directions: *Circle the things God has made for us.*

God cares for us by giving us all we need.

Family Note

Lesson 20: God Cares for Us and All He Has Made

The two stories for this lesson are adaptations of Matthew 6:26–34 and 18:10–14, and John 10:11–15. God is the source of all we have and all we need. He loves us. He wants to share his life with us now and he wants us to be with him someday in heaven. God has told us, shown us, and given us all that we need to be the best images of God we can be. Jesus told us that God takes care of all that he has made. We know God loves and takes care of us.

Vocabulary

Divine Providence: God's all-wise plan for all he has created and his loving care for all creation

Concepts of Faith

Who takes care of us always?
God takes care of us always.

Correspondence to the *Catechism of the Catholic Church*

God carries out his plan—divine providence: *CCC* 302–5, 320–23

Suggested Activity

Review the Guardian Angel Prayer with your child:

Angel of God,
my guardian dear,
to whom God's love commits me here,
ever this day be at my side,
to light and guard, to rule and guide.
Amen.

Directions: Circle the children who are caring for God's world.

We should take care of all that God has given us.

Family Note

Lesson 20: God Cares for Us and All He Has Made

The two stories for this lesson are adaptations of Matthew 6:26–34 and 18:10–14, and John 10:11–15. God is the source of all we have and all we need. He loves us. He wants to share his life with us now and he wants us to be with him someday in heaven. God has told us, shown us, and given us all that we need to be the best images of God we can be. Jesus told us that God takes care of all that he has made. We know God loves and takes care of us.

Vocabulary

Divine Providence: God's all-wise plan for all he has created and his loving care for all creation

Concepts of Faith

Who takes care of us always?
God takes care of us always.

Correspondence to the *Catechism of the Catholic Church*

God carries out his plan—divine providence: *CCC* 302–5, 320–23

Suggested Activity

Review the Guardian Angel Prayer with your child:

Angel of God,
my guardian dear,
to whom God's love commits me here,
ever this day be at my side,
to light and guard, to rule and guide.
Amen.

All Saints' Booklet

Saint Francis helped the sick and the poor.

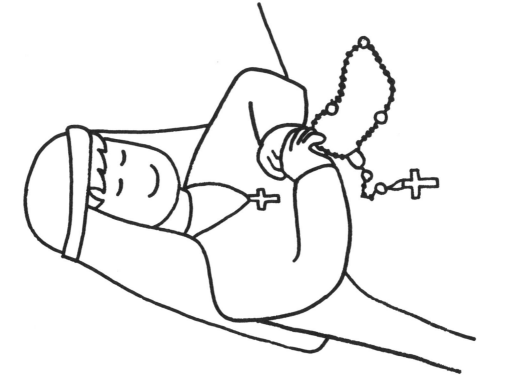

Saint Bernadette prayed the Rosary.

Family Note

Lesson 21: All Saints' Day

This lesson will introduce the children to All Saints' Day. On All Saints' Day we remember all the holy men and women who followed Jesus while they were living on earth. They tried always to act as images of God. Now the saints live with God in heaven. We go to Mass and ask the saints to pray for us.

Vocabulary

saints: holy men and women who followed Jesus and now live with God in heaven

Concepts of Faith

Who are the saints?

The saints are people who lived as images of God on earth and are now living in heaven with God.

Correspondence to the *Catechism of the Catholic Church*

The Church is holy: *CCC 823, 828*
The communion of saints: *CCC 946, 949*
The communion of the Church of heaven and earth: *CCC 956–57, 962*

Suggested Activity

Read your child a story about the life of a saint.

All Saints' Booklet

Saint Nicholas shared all he had with others.

Saint Anne was Mary's mother. She loved God and prayed to him.

All Saints' Booklet

Saint Thérèse did little things for others.

Saint John Bosco taught young boys about God.

Directions: Match the food to its shadow.

We thank God for all he has given us.

Family Note

Lesson 22: Thanksgiving

The story for this lesson is an adaptation of Luke 17:11–19. Thanksgiving is not just a time for a big meal with family and friends. It is a time for all God's family to join together to say "thank you" and to give praise to our loving Father who made all things. Through our prayers, we thank God for all he has given us. We also show God we are thankful by taking care of what he has given us.

Correspondence to the *Catechism of the Catholic Church*

Liturgical celebration: *CCC* 1145–62, 1189–92
Liturgical seasons: *CCC* 1163–65
Liturgical year: *CCC* 1168–71, 1194
Prayers of thanksgiving: *CCC* 2637–38, 2648

Suggested Activity

Recite the Grace before Meals with your child:

Bless us, O Lord, and these thy gifts,
which we are about to receive from thy bounty,
through Christ, our Lord. Amen.

Directions: Trace the letters.

We count the weeks of Advent.

Family Note

Lesson 23: First Week of Advent—Preparing Our Hearts and Homes

As we wait for the celebration of Jesus' birthday, Christmas, we prepare our homes, and more importantly, our hearts. During the waiting period, Advent, there are many ways in which we can show our love for God and others. It is important we share the true meaning of Christmas—that is, love—in our daily lives throughout the entire year and not just during this season.

Vocabulary

Advent: Coming; the time of waiting and getting ready to celebrate Jesus' birthday

Concepts of Faith

Who is Jesus?
Jesus is God the Son made man.

What do we do during Advent?
We wait for the coming of Jesus' birthday.

When do we celebrate Jesus' birthday?
We celebrate Jesus' birthday on Christmas.

Correspondence to the *Catechism of the Catholic Church*

Preparations for Christ's coming: *CCC 522–24*
Advent: *CCC 524, 1095*
Christmas mystery: *CCC 525–26, 563*
Mysteries of Jesus' infancy: *CCC 527–30*
Liturgical seasons: *CCC 1163–65*
Liturgical year: *CCC 1168–71, 1194*

Suggested Activity

Use an Advent wreath with your family to count the weeks until Christmas.

Directions: Draw a line from each item to where it belongs.

Advent is a time of preparing our hearts and homes for Jesus' birthday.

Family Note

Lesson 23: First Week of Advent—Preparing Our Hearts and Homes

As we wait for the celebration of Jesus' birthday, Christmas, we prepare our homes, and more importantly, our hearts. During the waiting period, Advent, there are many ways in which we can show our love for God and others. It is important we share the true meaning of Christmas—that is, love—in our daily lives throughout the entire year and not just during this season.

Vocabulary

Advent: Coming; the time of waiting and getting ready to celebrate Jesus' birthday

Concepts of Faith

Who is Jesus?
Jesus is God the Son made man.

What do we do during Advent?
We wait for the coming of Jesus' birthday.

When do we celebrate Jesus' birthday?
We celebrate Jesus' birthday on Christmas.

Correspondence to the *Catechism of the Catholic Church*

Preparations for Christ's coming: *CCC 522–24*
Advent: *CCC 524, 1095*
Christmas mystery: *CCC 525–26, 563*
Mysteries of Jesus' infancy: *CCC 527–30*
Liturgical seasons: *CCC 1163–65*
Liturgical year: *CCC 1168–71, 1194*

Suggested Activity

Use an Advent wreath with your family to count the weeks until Christmas.

Directions: Connect the dots. Trace the letters. Color the picture.

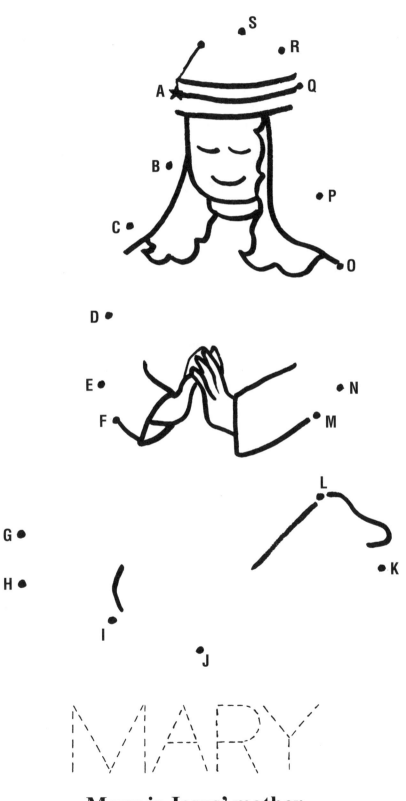

Mary is Jesus' mother.

Family Note

Lesson 24: Second Week of Advent—Mary Said "Yes" to God

The story for this lesson is an adaptation of Luke 1:26–45. Mary willingly chose to do what God asked her to do. Mary is an example for all people. She showed her love for God in all she thought, said, and did. We should follow her example. We ask Mary to pray for all of us so we will be more like her and her Son, Jesus.

Vocabulary

Advent: Coming; the time of waiting and getting ready to celebrate Jesus' birthday
angels: persons created by God without bodies. They praise God, act as God's messengers and our guardians.

Concepts of Faith

Who is Mary?
Mary is the Mother of God.

Who are the angels?
The angels are persons but they do not have bodies. They praise God, and act as God's messengers and our guardians.

Correspondence to the *Catechism of the Catholic Church*

Conceived by the power of the Holy Spirit: *CCC 484–86*
Born of the Virgin Mary: *CCC 487*
Mary's predestination: *CCC 488–89*
The Immaculate Conception: *CCC 490–93, 508*
"Let it be done to me according to your word…": *CCC 494*
Mary's divine motherhood: *CCC 495, 509*
Mary's virginity: *CCC 496–98*
Mary—"ever-virgin": *CCC 499–501, 510*
Mary's virginal motherhood in God's plan: *CCC 502–7, 511*
Preparations for Christ's coming: *CCC 522–24*
Advent: *CCC 524, 1095*
Christmas mystery: *CCC 525–56, 563*
Mysteries of Jesus' infancy: *CCC 527–30*
"Rejoice, you who are full of grace": *CCC 721–26, 744*
Mary—Mother of Christ, Mother of the Church: *CCC 963*
Wholly united with her Son: *CCC 964–65*
"… also in her Assumption": *CCC 966, 973–75*
"… she is our Mother in the order of grace": *CCC 967–70*
Devotion to the Blessed Virgin: *CCC 971*
Mary—Eschatological icon of the Church: *CCC 972*
The sanctoral in the liturgical year: *CCC 1172*
In communion with the holy Mother of God: *CCC 2676–77*

Suggested Activity

Recite the Hail Mary with your child:

Hail, Mary, full of grace, the Lord is with thee.
Blessed art thou among women, and blessed is the fruit of thy womb, Jesus.
Holy Mary, Mother of God, pray for us sinners now and at the hour of our death.
Amen.

Directions: Match what our mothers do to what Mary did.

Mary took care of Jesus the way our mothers take care of us.

Family Note

Lesson 24: Second Week of Advent—Mary Said "Yes" to God

The story for this lesson is an adaptation of Luke 1:26–45. Mary willingly chose to do what God asked her to do. Mary is an example for all people. She showed her love for God in all she thought, said, and did. We should follow her example. We ask Mary to pray for all of us so we will be more like her and her Son, Jesus.

Vocabulary

Advent: Coming; the time of waiting and getting ready to celebrate Jesus' birthday
angels: persons created by God without bodies. They praise God, act as God's messengers and our guardians.

Concepts of Faith

Who is Mary?
Mary is the Mother of God.

Who are the angels?
The angels are persons but they do not have bodies. They praise God, and act as God's messengers and our guardians.

Correspondence to the *Catechism of the Catholic Church*

Conceived by the power of the Holy Spirit: *CCC* 484–86
Born of the Virgin Mary: *CCC* 487
Mary's predestination: *CCC* 488–89
The Immaculate Conception: *CCC* 490–93, 508
"Let it be done to me according to your word…": *CCC* 494
Mary's divine motherhood: *CCC* 495, 509
Mary's virginity: *CCC* 496–98
Mary—"ever-virgin": *CCC* 499–501, 510
Mary's virginal motherhood in God's plan: *CCC* 502–7, 511
Preparations for Christ's coming: *CCC* 522–24
Advent: *CCC* 524, 1095
Christmas mystery: *CCC* 525–56, 563
Mysteries of Jesus' infancy: *CCC* 527–30
"Rejoice, you who are full of grace": *CCC* 721–26, 744
Mary—Mother of Christ, Mother of the Church: *CCC* 963
Wholly united with her Son: *CCC* 964–65
"… also in her Assumption": *CCC* 966, 973–75
"… she is our Mother in the order of grace": *CCC* 967–70
Devotion to the Blessed Virgin: *CCC* 971
Mary—Eschatological icon of the Church: *CCC* 972
The sanctoral in the liturgical year: *CCC* 1172
In communion with the holy Mother of God: *CCC* 2676–77

Suggested Activity

Recite the Hail Mary with your child:

Hail, Mary, full of grace, the Lord is with thee.
Blessed art thou among women, and blessed is the fruit of thy womb, Jesus.
Holy Mary, Mother of God, pray for us sinners now and at the hour of our death.
Amen.

Directions: Circle the things Joseph could make.

Joseph was a carpenter.

Family Note

Lesson 25: Third Week of Advent—Joseph, Jesus' Father on Earth

The story for this lesson is an adaptation of Matthew 1:18–25 and Luke 2:1–7. Joseph received special graces from God to be the head of the Holy Family. He was chosen by God to be Jesus' foster father and Mary's husband. Like Jesus and Mary, Joseph chose to obey the will of God in all things. He cared for Jesus and Mary out of love for them and for God.

Vocabulary

Holy Family: Jesus, the Blessed Virgin Mary, and Joseph
carpenter: person who builds and repairs things made out of wood

Concepts of Faith

Who was Joseph?
Joseph was Jesus' father on earth.

Who belongs to the Holy Family?
Jesus, the Blessed Virgin Mary, and Joseph belong to the Holy Family.

Correspondence to the *Catechism of the Catholic Church*

Annunciation of the angel to Joseph: *CCC* 497, 1846
Feast day of Saint Joseph: *CCC* 2177
Jesus' submission to Joseph: *CCC* 532
Mysteries of Jesus' infancy: *CCC* 527–30
Patron of a happy death: *CCC* 1014
Role and calling of Joseph: *CCC* 437

Suggested Activity

Help your child make a Christmas present for someone as a gift of love.

Directions: Circle the tools Joseph could use.

Joseph was Jesus' father on earth.
He made things out of wood.

Family Note

Lesson 25: Third Week of Advent—Joseph, Jesus' Father on Earth

The story for this lesson is an adaptation of Matthew 1:18–25 and Luke 2:1–7. Joseph received special graces from God to be the head of the Holy Family. He was chosen by God to be Jesus' foster father and Mary's husband. Like Jesus and Mary, Joseph chose to obey the will of God in all things. He cared for Jesus and Mary out of love for them and for God.

Vocabulary

Holy Family: Jesus, the Blessed Virgin Mary, and Joseph
carpenter: person who builds and repairs things made out of wood

Concepts of Faith

Who was Joseph?
Joseph was Jesus' father on earth.

Who belongs to the Holy Family?
Jesus, the Blessed Virgin Mary, and Joseph belong to the Holy Family.

Correspondence to the *Catechism of the Catholic Church*

Annunciation of the angel to Joseph: *CCC* 497, 1846
Feast day of Saint Joseph: *CCC* 2177
Jesus' submission to Joseph: *CCC* 532
Mysteries of Jesus' infancy: *CCC* 527–30
Patron of a happy death: *CCC* 1014
Role and calling of Joseph: *CCC* 437

Suggested Activity

Help your child make a Christmas present for someone as a gift of love.

Directions: Cut out the pictures. Put them in the correct order.

Family Note

Lesson 26: Fourth Week of Advent—Christmas Is Jesus' Birthday

The story for this lesson is an adaptation of Luke 2:1–18. Jesus teaches us that life is truly a celebration of love to be offered to God. On his birthday, we renew our commitment to a life of love and pray that our hearts be filled with the peace and love of the Christ child. Christmas is a worldwide celebration of love, the love God has for us and the love we have for God and others.

Vocabulary

Christmas: Jesus' birthday
manger: a box where food for animals is kept

Concepts of Faith

What is Christmas?
The feast day of the birth of Jesus.

Correspondence to the *Catechism of the Catholic Church*

Announcement to the shepherds: *CCC* 437
Christmas mystery: *CCC* 525–26, 563
Mysteries of Jesus' infancy: *CCC* 527–30

Suggested Activity

Help your child set up a Nativity scene in anticipation of Christmas.

Directions: Connect the dots.

Jesus was born in a stable.

Family Note

Lesson 26: Fourth Week of Advent—Christmas Is Jesus' Birthday

The story for this lesson is an adaptation of Luke 2:1–18. Jesus teaches us that life is truly a celebration of love to be offered to God. On his birthday, we renew our commitment to a life of love and pray that our hearts be filled with the peace and love of the Christ child. Christmas is a worldwide celebration of love, the love God has for us and the love we have for God and others.

Vocabulary

Christmas: Jesus' birthday
manger: a box where food for animals is kept

Concepts of Faith

What is Christmas?
The feast day of the birth of Jesus.

Correspondence to the *Catechism of the Catholic Church*

Announcement to the shepherds: *CCC 437*
Christmas mystery: *CCC 525–26, 563*
Mysteries of Jesus' infancy: *CCC 527–30*

Suggested Activity

Help your child set up a Nativity scene in anticipation of Christmas.

Lenten Coupon

I will show my love by

_____

_____

_____

_____

_____

**Lent is a time for preparing ourselves
for the joy and new life of Easter.**

Family Note

Lesson 27: Lent

During Lent we make sacrifices to offer to God. We "do without" things such as a favorite television show or treats. We give up something to show God we love him, and that he is most important to us. Jesus gave up his life for us because he loves us.

Vocabulary

Lent: the forty days of sacrifice and prayer before Easter
sacrifice: offering something to God as a sign of love

Concepts of Faith

What is Lent?

Lent is a time for preparing ourselves for the joy and new life, grace, of Easter.

Correspondence to the *Catechism of the Catholic Church*

Forms of penance in Christian life: *CCC* 1434–39
Sacrifice: *CCC* 2099–100
Lent: *CCC* 540, 1095, 1438
Jesus as our teacher and model of holiness: *CCC* 516, 519–21, 561
Christ's whole life as a self-offering to the Father: *CCC* 606–18, 621–23
Christ's redemptive Death in the divine plan of salvation: *CCC* 599–605, 619–20
Prayer to Jesus: *CCC* 2669

Suggested Activity

As a family, decide to do something during Lent that shows God you love him.

Directions: Choose one activity for each day during Lent. Color the egg after you have completed the activity.

Tell someone you love them.

Thank God for something.

Make your bed.

Draw a picture for someone.

Share a treat.

Pick up your clothes.

Be kind to someone.

Sing a happy song.

Wash the dishes.

Set the table.

Say something nice to a friend.

Make someone laugh.

Kiss someone you love.

Pick up your toys.

Dance a happy dance.

Share a toy.

Hug someone.

Say a special prayer.

Dust the furniture.

Sweep the floor.

There are forty days in Lent.

Family Note

Lesson 27: Lent

During Lent we make sacrifices to offer to God. We "do without" things such as a favorite television show or treats. We give up something to show God we love him, and that he is most important to us. Jesus gave up his life for us because he loves us.

Vocabulary

Lent: the forty days of sacrifice and prayer before Easter
sacrifice: offering something to God as a sign of love

Concepts of Faith

What is Lent?
Lent is a time for preparing ourselves for the joy and new life, grace, of Easter.

Correspondence to the *Catechism of the Catholic Church*

Forms of penance in Christian life: *CCC* 1434–39
Sacrifice: *CCC* 2099–100
Lent: *CCC* 540, 1095, 1438
Jesus as our teacher and model of holiness: *CCC* 516, 519–21, 561
Christ's whole life as a self-offering to the Father: *CCC* 606–18, 621–23
Christ's redemptive Death in the divine plan of salvation: *CCC* 599–605, 619–20
Prayer to Jesus: *CCC* 2669

Suggested Activity

As a family, decide to do something during Lent that shows God you love him.

Directions: Choose one activity for each day during Lent.
Color the egg after you have completed the activity.

- Tell someone you love them.
- Thank God for something.
- Make your bed.
- Draw a picture for someone.
- Share a treat.
- Pick up your clothes.
- Be kind to someone.
- Sing a happy song.
- Wash the dishes.
- Set the table.
- Say something nice to a friend.
- Make someone laugh.
- Kiss someone you love.
- Pick up your toys.
- Dance a happy dance.
- Share a toy.
- Hug someone.
- Say a special prayer.
- Dust the furniture.
- Sweep the floor.

Acts of love during Lent show our love for Jesus.

Family Note

Lesson 27: Lent

During Lent we make sacrifices to offer to God. We "do without" things such as a favorite television show or treats. We give up something to show God we love him, and that he is most important to us. Jesus gave up his life for us because he loves us.

Vocabulary

Lent: the forty days of sacrifice and prayer before Easter
sacrifice: offering something to God as a sign of love

Concepts of Faith

What is Lent?

Lent is a time for preparing ourselves for the joy and new life, grace, of Easter.

Correspondence to the *Catechism of the Catholic Church*

Forms of penance in Christian life: *CCC* 1434–39
Sacrifice: *CCC* 2099–100
Lent: *CCC* 540, 1095, 1438
Jesus as our teacher and model of holiness: *CCC* 516, 519–21, 561
Christ's whole life as a self-offering to the Father: *CCC* 606–18, 621–23
Christ's redemptive Death in the divine plan of salvation: *CCC* 599–605, 619–20
Prayer to Jesus: *CCC* 2669

Suggested Activity

As a family, decide to do something during Lent that shows God you love him.

Stations of the Cross Booklet

2. Jesus carries his Cross.

1. Pilate condemns Jesus.

Family Note

Lesson 27: Lent

During Lent we make sacrifices to offer to God. We "do without" things such as a favorite television show or treats. We give up something to show God we love him, and that he is most important to us. Jesus gave up his life for us because he loves us.

Vocabulary

Lent: the forty days of sacrifice and prayer before Easter
sacrifice: offering something to God as a sign of love

Concepts of Faith

What is Lent?

Lent is a time for preparing ourselves for the joy and new life, grace, of Easter.

Correspondence to the *Catechism of the Catholic Church*

Forms of penance in Christian life: *CCC* 1434–39
Sacrifice: *CCC* 2099–100
Lent: *CCC* 540, 1095, 1438
Jesus as our teacher and model of holiness: *CCC* 516, 519–21, 561
Christ's whole life as a self-offering to the Father: *CCC* 606–18, 621–23
Christ's redemptive Death in the divine plan of salvation: *CCC* 599–605, 619–20
Prayer to Jesus: *CCC* 2669

Suggested Activity

As a family, decide to do something during Lent that shows God you love him.

Stations of the Cross Booklet

4. Jesus meets his mother.

3. Jesus falls the first time.

Stations of the Cross Booklet

6. Veronica wipes Jesus' face.

5. Simon helps Jesus carry the Cross.

Stations of the Cross Booklet

8. Jesus meets the women of Jerusalem.

7. Jesus falls a second time.

Stations of the Cross Booklet

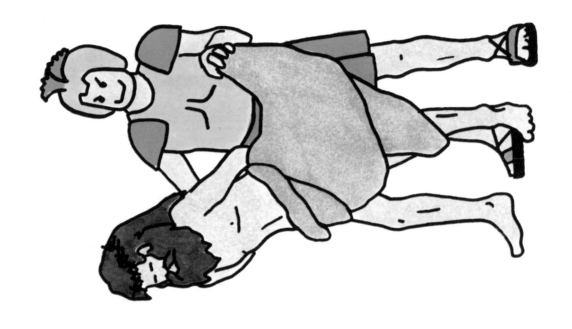

10. The soldiers take Jesus' clothes.

9. Jesus falls the third time.

Stations of the Cross Booklet

12. Jesus dies on the Cross.

11. Jesus is nailed to the Cross.

Stations of the Cross Booklet

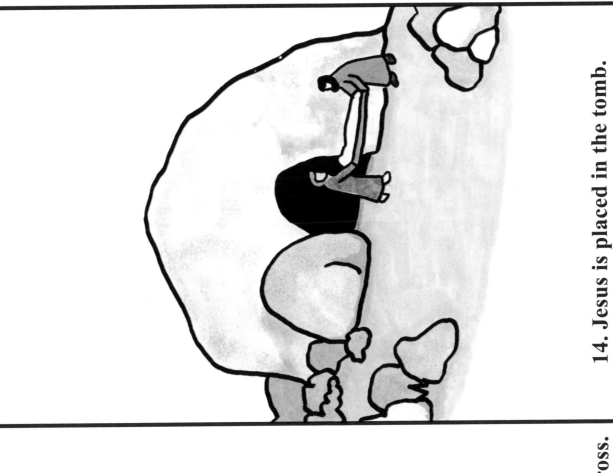

14. Jesus is placed in the tomb.

13. Jesus is taken down from the Cross.

Directions: Cut out the palm branches. Glue them onto the road.

The people waved palm branches.

Family Note

Lesson 28: Palm Sunday and Holy Week

Palm Sunday is the beginning of Holy Week. On the first Palm Sunday, Jesus entered Jerusalem amid the cheers and the praises of the people, a sharp contrast to what would happen to him at the end of this Holy Week.

Vocabulary

hosanna: a greeting of praise

Concepts of Faith

What happened on Palm Sunday?
Jesus entered Jerusalem amid shouts of praise.

Correspondence to the *Catechism of the Catholic Church*

Christ's redemptive Death in the divine plan of salvation: *CCC* 599–605, 619–20
Christ's whole life as a self-offering to the Father: *CCC* 606–18, 621–23
Jesus freely embraces the Father's redemptive love: *CCC* 609
Death of Christ as the unique and definitive sacrifice: *CCC* 613–14
Jesus substitutes his obedience for our disobedience: *CCC* 615
Jesus consummates his sacrifice on the Cross: *CCC* 616–17
Our participation in Christ's sacrifice: *CCC* 618

Suggested Activity

Show your child the palm branches given out at church. Tell your child the story of Jesus' triumphant entrance into Jerusalem.

Directions: Connect the dots. Color the picture.

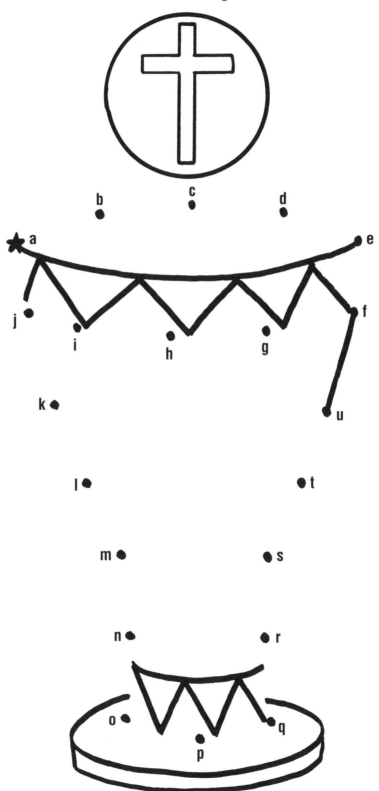

This is My Body. This is the chalice of My Blood.

Family Note

Lesson 28: Palm Sunday and Holy Week

Holy Week includes Palm Sunday, the day people sang Hosanna to Jesus; Holy Thursday, the day of the Last Supper; Good Friday, the day Jesus died; and Holy Saturday, the day Jesus' body lay in the tomb.

Vocabulary

hosanna: a greeting of praise

Concepts of Faith

What happened on Holy Thursday?
On Holy Thursday, Jesus and the Apostles shared the Last Supper, the first Mass.

What happened on Good Friday?
On Good Friday, Jesus died on the Cross.

Correspondence to the *Catechism of the Catholic Church*

Christ's redemptive Death in the divine plan of salvation: *CCC 599–605, 619–20*
Christ's whole life as a self-offering to the Father: *CCC 606–18, 621–23*
Jesus freely embraces the Father's redemptive love: *CCC 609*
Death of Christ as the unique and definitive sacrifice: *CCC 613–14*
Jesus substitutes his obedience for our disobedience: *CCC 615*
Jesus consummates his sacrifice on the Cross: *CCC 616–17*
Our participation in Christ's sacrifice: *CCC 618*

Suggested Activity

Show your child a picture of the Last Supper and a picture of Jesus on the Cross.

Directions: Cut out the pictures. Put them in the correct order.

Family Note

Lesson 28: Palm Sunday and Holy Week

Holy Week includes Palm Sunday, the day people sang Hosanna to Jesus; Holy Thursday, the day of the Last Supper; Good Friday, the day Jesus died; and Holy Saturday, the day Jesus' body lay in the tomb.

Vocabulary

hosanna: a greeting of praise

Concepts of Faith

What happened on Holy Thursday?
On Holy Thursday, Jesus and the Apostles shared the Last Supper, the first Mass.

What happened on Good Friday?
On Good Friday, Jesus died on the Cross.

Correspondence to the *Catechism of the Catholic Church*

Christ's redemptive Death in the divine plan of salvation: *CCC* 599–605, 619–20
Christ's whole life as a self-offering to the Father: *CCC* 606–18, 621–23
Jesus freely embraces the Father's redemptive love: *CCC* 609
Death of Christ as the unique and definitive sacrifice: *CCC* 613–14
Jesus substitutes his obedience for our disobedience: *CCC* 615
Jesus consummates his sacrifice on the Cross: *CCC* 616–17
Our participation in Christ's sacrifice: *CCC* 618

Suggested Activity

Show your child a picture of the Last Supper and a picture of Jesus on the Cross.

Directions: Trace the words and color the picture.

HE IS RISEN

Alleluia! He is risen.

Family Note

Lesson 29: Easter Sunday

Easter is the celebration of new life. At this time we remember Jesus' triumph over death, his Resurrection. Easter is the most joyous feast of the Church, celebrating the new life we receive from Jesus. We want to live with Jesus now, and someday we hope to be with him in heaven.

Vocabulary

Resurrection: when Jesus rose from the dead on the third day after he died on the Cross
tomb: a small cave where the body of Jesus was buried after he died on the Cross

Concepts of Faith

What happened on Easter Sunday?
On Easter Sunday, Jesus rose from the dead.

Correspondence to the *Catechism of the Catholic Church*

The liturgical year: *CCC* 1168–70

Suggested Activity

Go on a spring walk with your child. Look for signs of new life.

Our Father

Our Father who art in heaven,
hallowed be thy name.
Thy kingdom come.
Thy will be done on earth, as it is in heaven.
Give us this day our daily bread,
and forgive us our trespasses, as we forgive those who trespass against us,
and lead us not into temptation, but deliver us from evil.
Amen.

Apostles' Creed

I believe in God, the Father almighty,
Creator of heaven and earth,
and in Jesus Christ, his only Son, our Lord,
who was conceived by the Holy Spirit,
born of the Virgin Mary,
suffered under Pontius Pilate,
was crucified, died, and was buried;
he descended into hell;
on the third day he rose again from the dead;
he ascended into heaven,
and is seated at the right hand of God the Father almighty;
from there he will come to judge the living and the dead.
I believe in the Holy Spirit,
the holy catholic Church,
the communion of saints,
the forgiveness of sins,
the resurrection of the body,
and life everlasting.
Amen.

Glory Be

Glory be to the Father and to the Son and to the Holy Spirit,
as it was in the beginning is now, and ever shall be world without end.
Amen.

Hail Mary

Hail, Mary, full of grace, the Lord is with thee.
Blessed art thou among women and blessed is the fruit of thy womb, Jesus.
Holy Mary, Mother of God, pray for us sinners, now and at the hour of our death.
Amen.

Hail, Holy Queen

Hail, Holy Queen, Mother of Mercy,
our life, our sweetness and our hope.
To thee do we cry, poor banished children of Eve.
To thee do we send up our sighs,
mourning and weeping in this valley of tears.
Turn then, most gracious advocate,
thine eyes of mercy toward us,
and after this exile,
show unto us the blessed fruit of thy womb, Jesus.
O clement, O loving, O sweet Virgin Mary.
   V. Pray for us, O holy Mother of God.
   R. That we may be made worthy of the promises of Christ.

Memorare

Remember, O most gracious Virgin Mary,
that never was it known
that anyone who fled to thy protection,
implored thy help,
or sought thy intercession,
was left unaided.
Inspired by this confidence
I fly unto thee, O Virgin of virgins, my Mother.
To thee do I come, before thee I stand, sinful and sorrowful.
O Mother of the Word Incarnate.
despise not my petitions,
but in thy mercy hear and answer me.
Amen.

Angelus

The Angel of the Lord declared unto Mary.
And she conceived of the Holy Spirit.

Hail, Mary, . . .

Behold the handmaid of the Lord.
Be it done unto me according to thy word.

Hail, Mary, . . .

And the Word was made flesh.
And dwelt among us.

Hail, Mary, . . .

Pray for us, O holy Mother of God.
That we may be made worthy of the promises of Christ.
Let us pray:

Pour forth, we beseech thee, O Lord, thy grace into our hearts; that we, to whom the Incarnation of Christ, thy Son, was made known by the message of an angel, may by his Passion and Cross be brought to the glory of his Resurrection. Through the same Christ, our Lord. Amen.

Act of Contrition

My God,
I am sorry for my sins with all my heart.
In choosing to do wrong and failing to do good,
I have sinned against you
whom I should love above all things.
I firmly intend, with your help,
to do penance, to sin no more,
and to avoid whatever leads me to sin.
Our Savior Jesus Christ suffered and died for us.
In his name, my God, have mercy.
Amen.

An Act of Faith

O my God, I firmly believe that you are one God in three divine persons,
Father, Son, and Holy Spirit.
I believe that your divine Son became man and died for our sins
and that he will come to judge the living and the dead.
I believe these and all the truths which the Holy Catholic Church teaches
because you have revealed them who are eternal truth and wisdom,
who can neither deceive nor be deceived.
In this faith I intend to live and die.
Amen.

Morning Offering

O Jesus, through the Immaculate Heart of Mary,
I offer you my prayers, works, joys, and sufferings of this day
for all the intentions of your Sacred Heart,
in union with the Holy Sacrifice of the Mass throughout the world,
for the salvation of souls,
the reparation for sins,
the reunion of all Christians,
and in particular for the intentions of the Holy Father this month.
Amen.

Grace before Meals

Bless us, O Lord, and these thy gifts,
which we are about to receive from thy bounty,
through Christ our Lord. Amen.

Grace after Meals

We give thee thanks, for all thy benefits, Almighty God,
who live and reign forever.
[And may the souls of the faithful departed, through the mercy of God, rest in peace.]
Amen.

An Act of Hope

O Lord God, I hope by your grace
for the pardon of all my sins
and after life here to gain eternal happiness because you have promised it
who are infinitely powerful, faithful, kind, and merciful.
In this hope I intend to live and die.
Amen.

An Act of Love

O Lord God, I love you above all things
and I love my neighbor for your sake
because you are the highest, infinite and perfect good,
worthy of all my love.
In this love I intend to live and die.
Amen.

The Nicene Creed

I believe in one God,
the Father almighty, maker of heaven and earth,
of all things visible and invisible.

I believe in one Lord Jesus Christ,
the Only Begotten Son of God,
born of the Father before all ages.
God from God, Light from Light, true God from true God,
begotten, not made, consubstantial with the Father;
through him all things were made.
For us men and for our salvation
he came down from heaven,

[At the words that follow, up to and including "and became man", all bow.]
and by the Holy Spirit was incarnate of the Virgin Mary,
and became man.

For our sake he was crucified under Pontius Pilate,
he suffered death and was buried,
and rose again on the third day
in accordance with the Scriptures.
He ascended into heaven
and is seated at the right hand of the Father.
He will come again in glory to judge the living and the dead
and his kingdom will have no end.

I believe in the Holy Spirit, the Lord, the giver of life,
who proceeds from the Father and the Son,
who with the Father and the Son is adored and glorified,
who has spoken through the prophets.

I believe in one, holy, catholic and apostolic Church.
I confess one Baptism for the forgiveness of sins
and I look forward to the resurrection of the dead
and the life of the world to come. Amen.

NOTES

NOTES